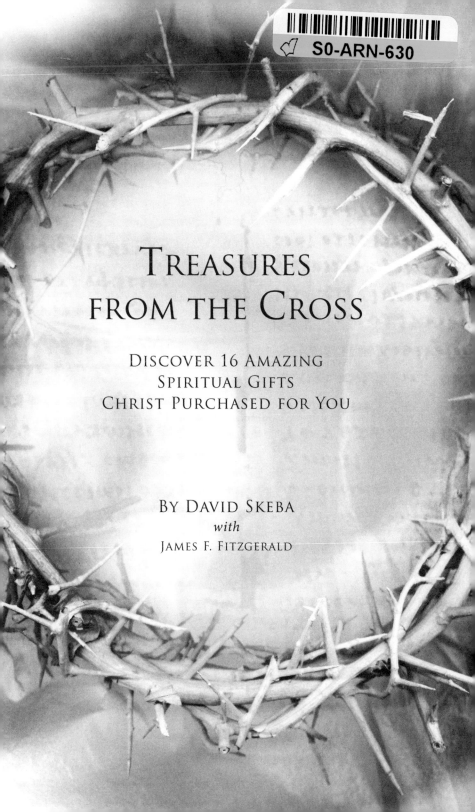

TREASURES FROM THE CROSS

DISCOVER 16 AMAZING
SPIRITUAL GIFTS
CHRIST PURCHASED FOR YOU

BY DAVID SKEBA

with

JAMES F. FITZGERALD

For questions or comments; to set up author interviews or speaking engagements; or to purchase this book or other biblical resources, please contact:

DISCOVER MINISTRIES

www.DiscoverMinistries.com
info@discoverministries.com
(866) 55 DISCOVER

DEDICATION

OLEEN EAGLE (1930-2007)—My aunt was a special woman of God who loved Jesus with all of her heart. She dedicated her life to allowing God to mold her into His character and to putting to death her sinful nature so that Christ could radiate from her life. Her faithful love, godly role model, wise counsel, impeccable integrity, and intercessory prayers helped bring me and my family to Jesus and impacted and enriched our Christian walk more than words can say. During her life, Oleen not only demonstrated how to live as a Christian, she also showed us how to die as one—with peace, anticipation, and unshakable faith in the reality of God and in the finished work of Christ on the cross.

SPECIAL ACKNOWLEDGEMENTS

Rev. Eugene Petroski, who was instrumental in helping me make my commitment to Christ and presented to me the reality of the Presence of God, and under whose pastoral leadership and teaching I learned the rich truths of the Bible.

Jim Fitzgerald, an author, a producer, and an entrepreneur whose insights and writing gifts helped greatly in creating this book. Jim has founded WatchWORD Productions, WatchWORD Worldwide, and TheBibleChannel.com to produce and distribute The WatchWORD Bible, a dynamic production of the New Testament as the world's first Videobook.

Mary Anne Skeba, my wonderful, talented wife who supported me throughout the process of writing this book and who designed the cover and created some of the illustrations.

The **Many Friends,** who provided wisdom and comments and helped to critique this material.

Megan Campanella, who provided editorial assistance (megan@ enucleoedits.com).

Jeff Hall, who provided the text design and layout, www.iongdw.com.

TABLE OF CONTENTS

INTRODUCTION

That they may come to know more fully God's great secret,
Christ Himself! For it is in Him, and in Him alone, that all
the treasures of wisdom and knowledge lie hidden.

Colossians 2:2-3 (Phillips)

THE mystery of the cross of Christ has always been difficult for me to understand. Perhaps you feel the same way. I used to think that it was just a tradition handed down to us by the church—without relevance for our generation in the twenty-first century.

As a result, I lived a period of my youth as if God did not exist… until one day I had a life-changing encounter with the God of the Bible and I began to see things differently. I discovered that He was indeed alive and that the Bible was indeed true.

Since then, during my forty years of being a Christian, the Holy Spirit has given me insights into the various aspects of the meaning of Christ's death on the cross. I have written this book because I am eager to help you discover its deeper meanings, just as I did—and not only to help you discover them, but to encourage you to go beyond the discovery to obtaining them and living a richer Christian life because of them.

Of all the information available today, an understanding of what occurred on the cross of Christ is more important than anything else we can ever know in our lifetime because it has eternal ramifications. It's sad to say, though, but most of us go through life without knowing the depth of God's passionate love for us. We really do not understand how much God desires to have a personal relationship with us and how much He wants us to be with Him for eternity. You can begin to experience this true love through the information presented in this book!

Why did the Father send His only Son to this earth? Why did Jesus endure such incredible, horrific suffering? What did He hope to accomplish? Christ desires that we understand this expression of His great love for us and that we comprehend the spiritual wealth He has lavished upon us as a result of His death and resurrection.

What Christ accomplished on the cross **can** be understood, but only through illumination by the Spirit of God.[1] Apart from the Holy Spirit's help, these truths will remain hidden from us, so ask God to enable you to grasp their full meaning.

Also be aware that Satan, the enemy of God and of man, does all within his power in the spiritual realm to keep us from discovering these truths.[2] Don't allow yourself to miss out on this vital information. Press on through any opposition and distractions and finish reading this book!

Each chapter will lead off with keynote Scriptures that highlight the final events of Christ's life—progressing from the Last Supper all the way up to His glorious resurrection—and will present a related treasure from the cross. Everything presented in this book is based on the fundamental truth that the Bible is the divinely inspired Word of God—the infallible revelation of God to man.[3]

In order to get the most out of this book, I encourage you to read one chapter per sitting. Look up and read each endnote Scripture reference located at the conclusion of each lesson, and then meditate on the information presented. Approaching the study in this manner will help you "unearth" spiritual treasures that you probably would not have found otherwise. Remember, hidden treasures are only discovered as we dig for them.

The precious treasures that Christ provided through the cross are extended to us as love gifts. Jesus paid the highest price possible to give us the most expensive gifts that we will ever be offered. Now imagine receiving a very lovely present and when you unwrap and open it, to your surprise, you find many individual smaller gifts beautifully wrapped inside. Similarly, the treasures from the cross are contained in the person of Christ.

But imagine leaving some of these gifts unopened. Who would do that? Yet this is what many Christians do with the gifts of Christ. For whatever reason, they fail to "open," or understand, all the treasures Jesus has obtained for them on the cross. As a result, because of this ignorance of all the victories He has won for them, they experience frustration and defeat in certain areas of their walk with God.

Although Jesus has already purchased these costly gifts for us, they are not automatically ours; we must receive them. In fact, these wonderful treasures do not become ours until we *receive* Christ Himself, as the Apostle John wrote: "*To all who received him, to those who believed in his name, he gave the right to become children of God.*"[4] Indeed, is any gift truly "ours" until we receive it?

It is my prayer that as you explore the contents of this book you will discover how much Christ really loves you and what He has achieved personally for you on the cross. And that it would lead to a life-changing encounter with the living Christ whereby you "receive Him" and ultimately enjoy fellowship with Him forever.

As you move forward in this book, you will get insight into the depth of **Christ's love**—a love so great that He would rather die an excruciating death than live in heaven without you.

You'll also gain a better comprehension of **God's ways**—ways so much higher, different, and foreign to our way of thinking as He provides a plan for a sinful human race to have fellowship with a just and holy God.

And finally, you'll learn **precisely what Jesus accomplished** for you by His death and resurrection.

These hidden treasures from the cross lie waiting to be discovered!

ENDNOTES

1. 1 Corinthians 2:10-14; Matthew 13:10-17
2. 2 Corinthians 4:3-4; Luke 8:5, 12
3. 2 Timothy 3:15-17; 2 Peter 1:20-21
4. John 1:12

CHAPTER 1

YOUR SIN COVERED:
ATONEMENT

For the life of a creature is in the blood, and I have given it to you to make atonement for yourselves on the altar; it is the blood that makes atonement for one's life.

Leviticus 17:11

This is how God showed his love among us: He sent his one and only Son into the world... as an atoning sacrifice for our sins.

1 John 4:9-10

AROUND 6,000 years ago, God created our first parents, Adam and Eve, to have fellowship with Him. He made them in His image, without sin, and with the ability to make their own choices. *"The man and his wife were both naked and they felt no shame."* [1]

God commanded them not to eat the fruit of a specific tree in the Garden of Eden in order to test their obedience. But when Adam and Eve ate the forbidden fruit, their sin of disobedience broke their fellowship with God and caused them to lose some form of their spiritual "clothing." [2] Suddenly they realized they were naked and they felt shame and tried to cover their nakedness.

In their pathetic efforts to clothe themselves and hide from God, Adam and Eve *"sewed fig leaves together and made coverings for themselves."*[3] This covering, produced by mere human effort, could not hide their sin and shame from God's sight. If their sin were to be covered, it had to be covered **God's way**—not man's way. Adam and Eve were incapable of doing it for themselves, just as we are.

From our human perspective, God faced a dilemma. He loved Adam and Eve with infinite love, yet He hated sin with infinite hatred. Furthermore, His holy character demanded that justice be satisfied, which involved a death penalty for sin. What could He do to be both just and merciful?

God's Way for Covering Human Sin

Even before God had created Adam and Eve, He devised a plan that the Bible calls *atonement*. Through atonement, God would meet His requirement for justice and yet, in love, save Adam, Eve, and the entire human race from destruction. In the Old Testament, one main meaning of *atonement* is "to cover over," as captured in the Hebrew word *kaphar*.

The Bible says, *"The Lord God made garments of skin for Adam and his wife and clothed them."*[4] Here we see God killing the first sacrifice for the purpose of atonement. By taking the lives and shedding the innocent blood of living animals, God provided a covering for Adam and Eve. This "blood covering" was wholly effective. It not only covered their nakedness and sin in God's sight and removed their guilt and shame, but it also mended their broken fellowship with God and satisfied His need for justice. Adam and Eve were unable to restore their relationship with God themselves. **God** did it for them, taking the first step!

And to this very day, man is the only part of God's creation that has to make and wear clothing—a symbolic reminder of our nakedness before God and our need for "covering."

There in the Garden of Eden, God instituted His plan for all generations to come—that of using the blood of animals to cover sin. From that point onward, the bloodshed of an innocent victim was necessary to provide the kind of covering that was acceptable to God. God then enlarged upon that sacrificial system some 2,500 years after Eden when He gave the Law to Moses on Mt. Sinai.

Does all of this mean that we serve a God who is some kind of bloodthirsty, sadistic butcher? Certainly not!

Author Dr. Alfred Cave gives this wonderful insight into God's plan of atonement. In effect, God would

> throw, so to speak, a veil over sin so dazzling [to His eye], that the veil, and not the sin was visible...not in the sense of rendering [sin] invisible to Jehovah, but in the sense of completely engrossing His sight with something else...of disarming [sin so it could not] arouse the righteous anger of God....Atonement meant so covering the sinner that his sin was invisible or non-existent in the sense that it could no longer come between him and his Maker.[5]

Simply put, to atone for sin is to cover sin from God's sight so that it loses its power to provoke His righteous anger.

Covering sin through atonement can be crudely illustrated by the image of covering a pile of maggot-infested garbage with an expensive piece of luxurious embroidered fabric. One's eyes would only behold the beautiful material, not the repulsive ugliness beneath it. Similarly, through the sacrifice of innocent animals, God would provide an attractive covering that would draw His attention away from our transgressions. Without this covering, however, God's justice would obligate Him to mete out judgment on the person who committed the sin.

ANIMAL SACRIFICES—
A SHORT-TERM SOLUTION

However, this Old Testament procedure of using the blood of specific animals to cover sin was insufficient to deal with sin permanently. The Bible states that *"it is impossible for the blood of bulls and goats to take away sins."*[6] These sacrifices would serve only for the **temporary** covering of sins for Old Testament believers.

In ancient Israel before Christ, these animal sacrifices were required to be repeated over and over again each time the Israelites committed sin. Also, once a year, on the Day of Atonement, the High Priest had to enter into the Holy of Holies (located first in the tabernacle and then later in the temple) and offer sacrifices for himself and then for the entire nation for those sins that were unconfessed and committed in ignorance. Being imperfect, these sacrifices failed to completely satisfy God's justice and only pointed to something greater to come.

What was it about the death of these animals offered up to God that made their blood covering so attractive to Him? Although we cannot fully comprehend or explain why blood offerings were pleasing to God, one of the main reasons centered on the fact that these animal sacrifices were designed to be a type, to foreshadow the perfect sacrifice of Jesus Christ and to portray the different facets of His work on the cross.[7]

As these animals were put to death throughout the Old Testament, the various distinctive features of their sacrifices ascended as a fragrance to God, reminding Him of the corresponding future work of His Son on the cross. Christ's great love, His humble condescension to planet Earth, and His voluntary offering of Himself in delight to do His Father's will are to God, the Father, an endless source of pleasure and satisfaction, for *"no one has greater love than the one who lays down his life for his friends."* [8]

Regarding the limitations of animal sacrifices, Professor Walter H. Beuttler explained it this way:

> An animal sacrifice could not provide a perfect atonement for fallen man because they were irrational creatures incapable of independent thought, a moral sense of responsibility, and the ability to choose to make deliberate acts [like voluntarily giving up their lives for another]....The work of atonement was not performed by the victim, but was done upon it, unconsciously and unwittingly by another....What gave animal sacrifices their efficacy, or their power to cover sin, was the perfect Sacrifice foreordained before the creation of the world. [9]

The Old Testament believers died, in faith, with their sins only temporarily covered as they placed their hope in the future sacrifice of "the seed of the woman" promised in Genesis 3:15. Jesus Christ was the only One in the universe who could qualify to atone for our sins—past, present, and future.

ATONEMENT IN THE NEW TESTAMENT

When Jesus finally arrived, the permanent solution to dealing with sin became a reality. God justified Old Testament believers in anticipation of Christ's work—on credit, so to speak—just as He justifies New Testament believers as we look back, by faith, to what Christ has already accomplished. Through Christ's sacrifice, the sins of the Old Testament believers were forever removed from God's sight—just as ours are today.

In the New Testament, the Scriptures declare Christ to be *"the Lamb of God, who takes away the sin of the world."*[10] It was the divine blood that flowed from Christ's body that became the ultimate perfect covering for our sins. It represents the voluntary pouring out of His sinless life as an offering for sin in order to save us all. This "costly, beautiful luxurious garment" is what captures God's attention instead of our repulsive sins. This is what is meant when it is said that our sins are "under His blood."

We ensure that our sins are put "under His blood" through repentance and confession. Then, when God sees the blood of His righteous Son, He no longer sees our sins. Those sins have lost their power to provoke God's anger because Jesus satisfied and appeased the Law and justice of God on the cross. Our confessed sins no longer demand God's judgment because they are not visible to Him.

It is not that our record of sins vanishes, as if our sins were never even committed. Instead, it is that God's reaction to them is appeased by the "beautiful garment" of Christ's sacrifice that is thrown over them. Our sins will no longer require a penalty of judgment, and God will remember our sins no more.[11]

As wonderful as the "sin covering" is as indicated by *atonement* in the Old Testament, the meaning of atonement takes on other meanings in the New Testament such as reconciliation with God.[12] In addition, the "covering" of atonement also relates to the new spiritual clothing in which we are dressed by God Himself through Christ. The New Testament believer is "covered over" with white clothing that God gives to those who will enter heaven.[13]

These white garments represent a purity and righteousness provided to the believer by Christ. As one hymn writer so aptly wrote, "Dressed in His righteousness alone, Faultless to stand before the throne."[14]

Through Christ, the believer will regain the spiritual covering that was lost in Adam. And in many ways, the believer in Christ is in a far better position than if Adam had never fallen! As Christian apologist Dave Hunt, once wrote, "God must have allowed sin to enter this world in order to further His ultimate purpose for mankind."[15]

Like the fig leaves our first parents used to try and cover themselves, our self-made efforts to attain righteousness in God's sight are but coverings of *"filthy rags,"* unacceptable in His sight.[16] They simply lack the atoning requirements of innocent sacrificial blood, which we are unable to give. We need to strip off these *"filthy rags"* and, by faith, cover our sins, guilt, and shame God's way, so that we might be made presentable in His sight.

Only those whose sins are covered by Christ's atonement on the cross are protected from the judgment God must pass upon sin. Once covered, our sins are forever removed from God's sight, never again to come between us and our Creator.

ATONEMENT—
A TREASURE FROM THE CROSS

ENDNOTES

1. Genesis 2:25
2. Genesis 3:1-19
3. Genesis 3:7
4. Genesis 3:21
5. Myer Pearlman, *Knowing the Doctrines of the Bible,* Gospel Publishing House (Springfield, Missouri, 1937), 203.
6. Hebrews 10:1-4, 11
7. Colossians 2:16-17; Hebrews 8:1-5; 10:1
8. John 15:13; Genesis 8:20-21; Exodus 29:15-18; Leviticus 2:1-2; Ephesians 5:2; Philippians 4:14-19
9. Walter Beuttler, from his study notes on *The Offerings,* 1.
10. John 1:29
11. Hebrews 8:12; 10:15-18
12. Romans 3:25
13. Isaiah 61:10; Revelation 3:4-6; 6:9-11; 7:9-14; Galatians 3:26-27
14. *The Solid Rock* by Edward Mote, 1834; see Jude 1:24.
15. Dave Hunt, *The Berean Call* (September 2002), 1.
16. Isaiah 64:6

HISTORICAL INSIGHT INTO THE CRUCIFIXION

In determining a timeline for the final hours of Christ's life, it is important to understand that there were two different ways in which the days were divided back then: the Gentile (or Roman) way and the Jewish way.

The Romans divided their days from midnight to midnight, as we do today.

The Jews, however, began their twenty-four-hour days at sundown, or 6 p.m. Their days were patterned after how God created the original days, as recorded in the first chapter of Genesis: *"And there was evening, and there was morning."*

The Jews' first twelve hours of night were divided into four periods, called **"watches"**:

1st watch, or *"evening"*: 6 p.m. to 9 p.m. (see Mark 13:35)

2nd watch, or *"midnight"*: 9 p.m. to midnight

3rd watch, or *"cock-crow"*: Midnight to 3 a.m.

4th watch, or *"dawn"*: 3 a.m. to 6 a.m.

Their daytime was commonly divided into four periods, called **"hours"**:

"1st hour" (early morning): 6 a.m. to 9 a.m.

"3rd hour": 9 a.m. to noon

"6th hour": Noon to 3 p.m.

"9th hour": 3 p.m. to 6 p.m.

The gospels of Matthew, Mark, and Luke express the time of day in this Jewish way. John, however, tends to use the Roman method, especially in John 19:14 (i.e., *"the sixth hour"* means 6 a.m.).

Since the people only had shadows and positions of the sun to work with, and no way to measure precise time as we do, their reference to the time of day is an approximation at best. Therefore, it stands to reason that people gave a general reference to the time of day by estimating time to be around the specific "watch" or "hour" periods.

CHAPTER 2

CHRIST TOOK YOUR PLACE:
SUBSTITUTION

Then came the day of Unleavened Bread on which the Passover lamb had to be sacrificed. Jesus sent Peter and John, saying, "Go and make preparations for us to eat the Passover."...

When the hour came, Jesus and His apostles reclined at the table. And He said to them, "I have eagerly desired to eat this Passover with you before I suffer. For I tell you, I will not eat it again until it finds fulfillment in the kingdom of God."...

And he took bread, gave thanks and broke it, and gave it to them, saying, "This is my body given for you; do this in remembrance of me." In the same way, after the supper he took the cup, saying, "This cup is the new covenant in my blood, which is poured out for you."

Luke 22:7-8, 14-16, 19-20

WE discovered in the previous chapter how God, taking the first step, restored mankind back to Himself by providing the first sacrifice. From the very beginning, God demonstrated to fallen humanity that the only way to approach Him was through faith in the sacrificial shedding of blood of an innocent victim.

The underlying principle of sacrifice is substitution, which was an integral part of God's plan of atonement. It is an exchange—a life given for a life, an innocent victim giving up its life in order to save another.

Why is substitution necessary? Because God's holy and righteous character requires that a death penalty be paid for sin. We humans find ourselves in mortal danger because we are sinners and guilty of transgressing God's moral laws. Therefore, we sinners must die. However, God, in His mercy, provided for substitution to save us from terrible judgment. He would permit another to take our place.

THE FOUR PRINCIPLES OF SUBSTITUTION

In the Old Testament God's great plan of substitution consisted of four basic principles:

1. Sinful people, by faith, confessed their sins and transferred them onto designated innocent animals.[1]

2. God's judgment fell upon these substitutes as their lifeblood was shed and their bodies burned in the fire.

3. God accepted the death of the innocent victims as payment for sin in place of the lives of the people, allowing them to escape His judgment.

4. In turn, the life and innocence of the substitutes were transferred to the sinners, who received them by faith. God justified them—treating them just as if they had never committed those sins.

As we shall see, the principles behind these four points also apply in the New Testament. We may not fully understand, or even like, this unusual and bloody way that God chose to remove our sins, but if

we desire to unload the sin from off of us and live, we have no other alternative.

By transferring their sins onto the sacrificial animals, the people were forgiven and their fellowship with God was reestablished. If they failed to transfer their sins, however, the sin would remain upon them, keeping them alienated from God. This plan of substitution made it possible for God to be both just and gracious.

We also learned in the previous chapter that this Old Testament system of animal sacrifices was only an imperfect and temporary solution.[2] What gave these sacrifices their power was that they pointed ahead toward Christ's great work on the cross, portraying all of the foreshadows of His substitutionary death. In fact, Jesus died on the same day of the Jewish Passover, and we believe He even died at the same time that the Passover lamb was traditionally sacrificed. Jesus is God's sinless Lamb—THE perfect, sinless, and final substitute for everyone's sins.[3]

AN ILLUSTRATION OF SUBSTITUTION

The principle of substitution can be illustrated by the story of a powerful king who, over a period of time, learned that many valuable things were being stolen from his palace. Outraged, the king issued this royal decree: "The thief, when caught, will be severely whipped." But despite his proclamation, the stealing continued.

Finally the thief was caught one evening and brought before the king. One look at the thief sent shivers down the king's spine. To his astonishment and dismay, the thief turned out to be his own daughter. The king's subjects watched intently to see what he would do. Would his love prevail over his justice? Would he break his word and show preferential treatment to his daughter? Or would he keep his word and have her whipped?

"The punishment must be carried out," he proclaimed. "Tie her to the whipping post!" When the servants had finished binding her, the soldier took hold of the whip and positioned himself to deliver the first of many blows.

A silence settled over the courtyard where a large crowd had gathered. Then, unexpectedly, the king stood up from his throne and cried out, "Wait!" All eyes were fixed upon him as they watched him walk over to where his daughter was bound. What was he going to do—change his mind and spare her?

To the amazement of all there, the king removed his royal robes and wrapped his strong, loving arms around her—embracing her from behind. The crowd gasped in utter disbelief. Then he gave the order and accepted the lashes that had been meant for his daughter. In the same way that the king took the lashes for his daughter, Christ bore the sin payment for us.

A criminal in Christ's day, named Barabbas, also experienced this principle of substitution.

> As he sat in his prison cell awaiting execution for murder, a cold chill must have swept over him as he heard the crowd cry, "Barabbas, Barabbas!" Then he heard footsteps. A key grated in the lock. The door swung open....But to his astonishment he was released. He was free! A man named Jesus had taken his place. [4]

Barabbas was the only person who could ever say that Jesus Christ physically took his place on the cross. However, in a very real way, Christ did the same thing for every person ever born—past, present, and future.

Christ, who was innocent, loved us so much that He voluntarily became our substitute.[5] We should have been the ones to suffer and die for our own sins, but He willingly suffered our penalty for sin so that our sins could be transferred from ourselves and onto Him.

Reader, please take this very seriously. If you refuse to transfer your sins onto Christ, your sins will remain upon you, and you will leave God no other choice but to bring His judgment upon you.[6] Someone has to die for sin. And God has made a way through His Son so that it doesn't have to be you!

When we trust Christ, we [like Barabbas] will also walk out of the prison house of death and step into the bright sunlight of forgiveness and freedom. What an amazing truth! Christ died for me. He took my place![7]

This is what happens when we apply Christ's substitutionary work to our lives. It is as if we ourselves accompanied Christ as He was put to death [8] and went into the grave.[9] Furthermore, it is as if we came out of the grave with Him, being raised from the dead,[10] to live in heaven and forever enjoy unbroken fellowship with God.

SUBSTITUTION—
A TREASURE FROM THE CROSS

ENDNOTES

1. Leviticus 1:1-5; 16:21-22
2. Hebrews 8:5-13; Colossians 2:16-17
3. 1 Peter 1:18-20; Isaiah 53:5-6
4. David C. Egnar, *Our Daily Bread,* © Radio Bible Class, March 30, 1988. Used by permission.
5. John 10:14-18, 18:1-6; Matthew 26:53-54; also see Genesis 22:1-14.
6. Genesis 4:2-7
7. David C. Egnar, *Our Daily Bread.*
8. Galatians 2:20
9. Romans 6:4
10. Colossians 3:1

HISTORICAL INSIGHT INTO THE CRUCIFIXION

Let us sketch the probable timeline of Christ's final hours on the fifteenth day of the Jewish month Nisan, using their method of configuring a day—6 p.m. to 6 p.m.—as well as their "watch" and "hour" sections of the day. (*Locate the number to the left of each event below on the map on the next page. Follow the arrows to retrace Christ's footsteps.*)

Event	Approximate Time
1. Passover meal with the disciples (Upper Room)	1st watch into the 2nd watch
2. In the Garden of Gethsemane	2nd into the 3rd watch
2. Betrayal by Judas and Christ's arrest	3rd watch
3. Preliminary trial before Annas, the high priest	3rd watch – John 18:12-13, 24
3. Trial at residence of Caiaphas, the high priest	3rd into the 4th watch
3. Peter's denial of Christ	3rd watch – John 18:27
4. Final trial before the Jewish Sanhedrin	1st hour – Luke 22:66
5. Jesus taken to Pontius Pilate, the Roman procurator	1st hour – John 18:28; 19:14
6. Pilate sends Jesus to King Herod	1st hour – Luke 23:6-7
5. Jesus returned to Pilate for final verdict	1st hour – Luke 23:11
5. Jesus scourged	1st hour – Mark 15:25
7. Jesus crucified	3rd hour (9 a.m.) – Mark 15:25
7. Darkness enveloped the land until the 9th hour	6th hour (Noon) – Luke 23:44-45
7. Jesus died	9th hour (3 p.m.) – Mark 15:34-37

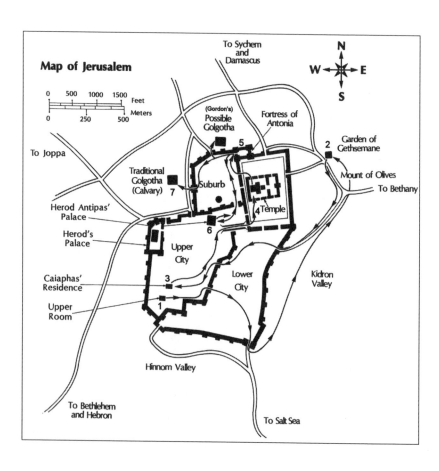

CHAPTER 3

A RIGHT STANDING WITH GOD:
RIGHTEOUSNESS

Then Jesus went with his disciples to a place called Gethsemane, and he said to them, "Sit here while I go over there and pray." He took Peter and the two sons of Zebedee along with him, and he began to be sorrowful and troubled. Then he said to them, "My soul is overwhelmed with sorrow to the point of death. Stay here and keep watch with me."

Going a little farther, he fell with his face to the ground and prayed, "My Father, if it is possible, may this cup be taken from me. Yet not as I will, but as you will."

Matthew 26:36-39

An angel from heaven appeared to him and strengthened him. And being in anguish, he prayed more earnestly, and his sweat was like drops of blood falling to the ground.

Luke 22:43-44

Let us fix our eyes on Jesus, the author and perfecter of our faith, who for the joy set before Him endured the cross, scorning its shame.

Hebrews 12:2

THE greatest need a sinner has is to be made righteous before God. The great plan of substitution, devised and agreed upon by both the Father and the Son before the world began,[1] was intended to do just that—to make sinners righteous before God.

Jesus could take our sins upon Himself as our substitute only because He was sinless. That is why no human being could ever save himself, let alone his fellow man. Every human being born into this world has descended from Adam and has inherited Adam's sinful nature[2]—with one exception: Jesus, the God-man!

God's plan to rescue mankind was to insert His sinless Son into the human race in order to give us a right standing before God. He did this through the virgin birth.[3] Christ's birth involved the Holy Spirit and a human mother, but not a human father. Therefore, He did not inherit Adam's sinful nature. In this way God could send a sinless Savior to bear our sins and to provide His righteousness to us. What an extravagant gift!

But in the Garden of Gethsemane, the human side of Jesus began to struggle with His mission. What was it that caused Jesus such anguish in His decision to "drink the cup" His Father offered Him? What did that cup contain that made the Son of God draw back in horror and overwhelming sorrow?

Do you think it was the experience of physical pain and suffering that lay ahead of Him? Yes, Jesus knew the physical pain would be terrible, beyond description. But the cup contained something that Jesus, the eternal Son of God, surely dreaded even more.

As the second person of the Trinity, Jesus abhorred sin with an absolute hatred. The perfect God-man had never known what it was like to commit a sin or defile His sinless life with anything unholy, let alone experience sin's filthy degradation. Now, taking upon Himself the wretched sins of all mankind throughout all history, He would actually **become sin for us**—something contrary to His very nature!

What Did the "Cup" Contain?

The cup that Jesus was horrified to drink was laced with the violence and the perversions of the sins of the entire human race—past, present, and future. By drinking it, Jesus would then know the guilt and shame of sin—its ugly repulsiveness and its horrible consequences!

While His disciples slept, Jesus wrestled in prayer about this monumental decision. Looking into this dreadful cup, Christ saw...

...A father kill his three children and wife of ten years and then take his own life. *There's murder in the cup.*

...Thousands drop to their knees and bow with their faces to the ground as they worship the image of their false god. *There's idolatry in the cup.*

...A pimp entice and entrap a boy and use him for financial gain in the human trafficking sex industry. *There's enslavement in the cup.*

...A couple resort to stealing so that they can continue injecting needles into their veins in order to make it through another hopeless day. *There's addiction in the cup.*

...A married man secretly enter the forbidden bed of his neighbor. *There's adultery in the cup.*

As Jesus continued to gaze into the cup with abhorrence, there was more. He saw...

...A young suicide bomber walk into a crowded downtown area and kill innocent men, women, and children. *There's terrorism in the cup.*

...A seductive woman lure passersby to have sex for money. *There's prostitution in the cup.*

...A minister's character and reputation irreparably damaged by someone's gossip and malice. *There's slander in the cup.*

...A pedophile kidnap a young girl, molest her, and then bury her alive. *There's sexual perversion in the cup.*

...An intoxicated driver walk away from a car accident, leaving behind the dead bodies of a woman's husband and only child. *There's drunkenness in the cup.*

More nauseating, horrendous scenes persisted unrelentingly in the cup, fueling Christ's astonishment and disgust.

...A coven of witches meets secretly under the full moon to conjure up demonic spirits and invoke them to do their bidding. *There's witchcraft in the cup.*

...A teenager takes his life, causing indescribable, lifelong heartache to his parents and family. *There's suicide in the cup.*

...A businessman embezzles hundreds of thousands of dollars from his company. *There's greed and theft in the cup.*

...A perverted father takes his daughter and performs his lustful will on her innocent body. *There's incest in the cup.*

As Christ continued to stare into the cup in anguish and revulsion, more scenes unfolded before Him, scenes of violence, injustice, oppression, deceitfulness, unfaithfulness, and occult involvement.[4]

All this evil was as contrary to Christ's holy, sinless character as night is from day, and it filled Him with dread to the core of His being.

Still there was yet one more dreadful ingredient contained in the cup—much worse than all the sin that Jesus had just seen. It was receiving God's wrath and being separated from His Father. Jesus and His Father had always been *one*, in perfect fellowship throughout eternity. Christ had never known a moment without this relationship with His Father. By becoming sin for us, however, Jesus would lose His eternal oneness with God. For a time, Christ would be separated from His Father, just like any sinner!

Is it any wonder that Jesus agonized so? Can we see now why He drew back? Who can fathom the depth of Christ's physical suffering? Being sinners, we are unable to grasp the holiness of God, so how can we even *begin* to comprehend the unbelievably greater suffering Jesus endured for us spiritually?

Doesn't it seem strange to you that the sin humanity so enjoys makes Christ recoil in horror? We must begin to see sin as God sees it and despise it like He does. Not until we truly realize what our sin did to Jesus can we really understand how evil sin is.

It is significant that all of this took place in Gethsemane, whose name means "oil-press." It was as if all the sins of the world were being pressed out and dripped into the cup Christ drank, much as oil is pressed out of an olive. In His final moments in Gethsemane, Christ continued to contemplate the contents of the cup. Every single sin ever committed, from individual acts to the murder of millions in concentration camps, became part of the concoction that filled the cup Jesus was asked to drink.

Added to this ungodly mixture were the spiritual demonic attacks He would endure, the betrayal and desertion, the hatred and rejection, the shame and humiliation, the mocking, the scourging, the spittle, the nails, the thorns, and the physical pain and suffering of the cross.

And the most terrifying ingredient of all: separation from His Father as a sinner!

CHRIST SUBMITS TO THE CUP

God is a God of infinite knowledge and possibilities. Surely there could have been another way to deal with the problem of sin other than having His Son die in our place on the cross. Jesus earnestly prayed three times that if it were possible, would His Father consider another way and exempt Him from going to the cross? Having reviewed every possibility, His Father said that this was the **only** way—His **best** way of dealing with human sin.

Christ's sinless nature recoiled at the horror of drinking this cup and becoming our sin bearer. The Bible tells us just how intense the struggle was within Him. The experience was so traumatic that it caused Him to sweat great drops of blood (*hematidrosis* is the actual medical term), and Jesus needed an angel to strengthen Him.[5]

Jesus knew that He was the only One who could rescue and deliver man from the eternal penalty for sin. If He chose not to partake of the cup, He would fail every Old Testament believer who had died in faith believing God's promise about Him. If He refused to drink the cup, all mankind would be hopelessly doomed. If He declined to consume it, He would disappoint His Father and not fulfill His plan, which was crafted before the creation of the world.

Yet as He looked ahead, beyond the cross, He saw multitudes of those whom He would save from destruction and bring into the family of God. He saw the eternal bliss that this temporary moment of agony would produce—and it filled Him with joy![6]

Heaven held its collective breath while the battle raged amid the olive trees below. Finally, after an hour of intense struggle, Christ made His decision. With trembling hands, He lifted the cup and pressed it to His lips, the bitter contents flooding His being.[7]

Only His love for His Father, the burning desire to do His Father's will, and His passionate love for us moved Him to drink the bitterness contained in that cup—being fully aware of all that it would cost Him.

The Bible tells us that God made Jesus *"who had no sin to be sin for us, so that in Him we might become the righteousness of God."*[8] Jesus never deserved to die because He was absolutely sinless.[9] The Scriptures are clear: Only the soul that sins shall die.[10] Yet Jesus **chose** to be an offering for sin. He willingly put Himself in that position so that He could offer His righteousness to us.

From the moment you repent and transfer your sins, by faith, onto Jesus your sin bearer, God the Father forgives you and transfers Christ's righteousness to you. This means that, in exchange for your faith in

Christ's work for you on the cross, His righteousness is put into your spiritual account, so to speak, much the same way as if someone deposited a great treasure into your earthly bank account. It then becomes yours![11]

As we continue to repent of our sins and trust in Christ, it is the righteousness of Christ that will give us entrance into heaven. It is a gift of God's grace, not of our good works, so that none of us can take any credit.[12]

RIGHTEOUSNESS— A TREASURE FROM THE CROSS

ENDNOTES

1. 1 Peter 1:19-20; Revelation 13:8
2. Romans 5:12; Psalm 51:5; Genesis 8:21
3. Matthew 1:22-25; Isaiah 7:14
4. Adapted from Dan Betzer, "The Wonder of Gethsemane," *The Pentecostal Evangel* (Gospel Publishing House, April 8, 1990), 12-13.
5. Luke 22:43-44
6. Hebrews 12:2
7. Dan Betzer
8. 2 Corinthians 5:21
9. Hebrews 4:15
10. Ezekiel 18:4
11. Romans 3:21-23; 4:18-25; 5:19; 10:3-4; Philippians 3:8-9; Hebrews 10:14
12. Ephesians 2:8-9; Romans 4:4-9

MEDICAL INSIGHT INTO THE CRUCIFIXION

Hematidrosis is a medical term for "bloody sweat." A very rare phenomenon, it is caused when, under conditions of great emotional stress, tiny capillaries in the sweat glands rupture, thereby mixing blood with perspiration.[1] "As a result of this hemorrhage...the skin becomes fragile and tender," which would have made Christ's upcoming physical beatings even more painful. There are differences of opinion as to Christ's actual blood loss, but it was probably minimal.[2] "Acute fear and intense mental contemplation were found to be the most frequent inciting causes" in seventy-six cases of hematidrosis that were studied and categorized during the latter part of the 1990s.[3]

1. R. Lumpkin, "The Physical Suffering of Christ," *Journal of Medical Association of Alabama,* 47 (1978): 8-10.

2. William D. Edwards, M.D., Wesley J. Gabel, M. Div., Floyd E. Hosmer, M.S., AMI, "On the Physical Death of Jesus Christ," *Journal of the American Medical Association* (March 21, 1986): 1456.

3. J. E. Holoubek, A. B. Holoubek, "Blood, Sweat, and Fear: A Classification of Hematidrosis," *Journal of Medicine,* 27 (1996) [3-4]: 115-33.

CHAPTER 4

YOUR RELATIONSHIP WITH GOD RESTORED:
RECONCILIATION

*Then Pilate announced to the chief priests and the crowd, "I
find no basis for a charge against this man."*

*But they insisted, "He stirs up the people all over Judea by
his teaching. He started in Galilee and has come all the way
here." On hearing this, Pilate asked if the man was a Galilean.
When he learned that Jesus was under Herod's jurisdiction, he
sent him to Herod, who was also in Jerusalem at that time.*

*When Herod saw Jesus, he was greatly pleased, because for a long
time he had been wanting to see him. From what he had heard
about him, he hoped to see him perform some miracle....Then
Herod and his soldiers ridiculed and mocked him. Dressing him
in an elegant robe, they sent him back to Pilate. That day Herod
and Pilate became friends—before this they had been enemies.*

Luke 23:4-12

WHEN Pontius Pilate heard the word *Galilee* as Jesus stood
before him, he must have been relieved. The fact that Jesus
was a Galilean provided an escape route for Pilate; it was Herod's job,
not his, to make the tough decision about what to do with Jesus!

Jesus was delivered to Herod—but then He was sent back to Pilate. And in that transfer, something unusual transpired in the two leaders' relationship. They moved from a state of being enemies to a state of being friends.

Pilate and Herod had been enemies of each other, but they were also enemies of God—just like you and me! But you might say, "I'm not in the same class as they are. My sins are nothing when compared to their wickedness." The Bible, however, clearly states that ever since Adam passed sin down to his descendants, all of us are by nature sinners and enemies of God.[1]

Being sinners by nature, we automatically produce sin in our lives. *Sin* means "missing the mark." In other words, God has a "mark," or a target, to hit—a standard for us to live up to. We all have missed the mark for which God originally intended in creating us—namely, to reflect His image and character and to serve Him by doing His will.[2]

Instead, sin caused separation from a holy God, and even hostility toward Him. When we sin we behave like Satan, the originator of sin, and we exhibit a character that is the opposite of God's.[3] This behavior makes us enemies of God as we continue to elevate our will above God's and live in rebellion to His authority.

Because of sin, there is nothing we can do on our own to overcome this enmity and establish a right relationship with God. We know that heathen worshippers try to appease their capricious and vindictive gods with gifts and offerings, to bribe them into a good disposition toward them; however, the God of the Bible cannot be appeased this way. He is not an ill-tempered god who needs to be placated for his angry disposition.

Rather, the God of the Bible is a God of infinite justice and holiness. We cannot get on good terms with Him through our own bargaining and efforts. We are unholy sinners incapable of meeting God's absolute standards.

Yet the Bible tells us that God is also infinitely merciful and gracious. Desiring our fellowship, He, the offended One, took the initiative to reconcile us to Himself. If He had not done this, there would have been no hope of reconciliation at all.

Christ—Our Bridge to God

To end the hostility, God sent His Son to die for sin on the cross. In His death, Jesus accepted the blame for our sins, even though He was not at fault. He did so to bring us back to God and to reestablish relationship with us. Christ's sacrifice removed the obstacle of sin, which stood between God and man like a chasm, by fully satisfying the legal requirements for our salvation. Therefore, this sacrifice of appeasement,[4] or what the Bible calls *propitiation*,[5] turned away God's righteous anger toward sin. Now our reconciliation has become possible.

The chasm of sin that existed between God and mankind can be illustrated by the story of two Indian tribes in America's Northern Great Plains.

The Teton and Kiowa Indian tribes had been enemies for decades. The Tetons settled on top of the northern ridge of one mountain range, and the Kiowas settled on the tree-covered southern range parallel to them. A steep gorge separated the two tribes.

Neither clan could attack the other by traveling from one mountaintop to the other. The rough terrain at the bottom of the fifty-mile gorge was impassable throughout its entire length, and the sides of the cliffs were steep and rocky. They would occasionally taunt and shoot arrows at each other across the expanse of the sixty-foot gorge, but they never engaged in hand-to-hand combat.

One day a missionary named Travis passed through on his way to Oregon, and Chief White Eagle of the Kiowa tribe gave him lodging for a few days. During his stay, the missionary prayed for a way to share the good news of Christ with them in a way they could understand, but he had a difficult time thinking of how to communicate it.

Two days after the missionary had arrived at the Kiowa tribe, a severe thunderstorm rocked the area in the middle of the night. The wind howled and lightning lit up the sky like fireworks. The noise was terrifying. The inhabitants stayed huddled in their tepees as they were afraid to come out.

At daybreak, Chief White Eagle and the missionary were the first ones up to see what damage the storm had caused. They noticed that the tall tree that used to be near the edge of the cliff was no longer standing. To their amazement, the tree had fallen across one of the narrowest points between the two ridges—creating a bridge between the two tribes for the very first time!

When the missionary realized the biblical relevance of what had happened, he quickly took advantage of the opportunity to share this with the leader: "Chief White Eagle, just as this gorge separated your tribe and the Tetons, who are enemies, so too was there a chasm between God and mankind due to sin. But Jesus Christ, God's Son, was struck dead by God as He took the penalty for our sin, and He became the bridge of reconciliation between sinful man and a holy God."

Soon thereafter, Hotah, the youngest son of Chief Big Elk, the Teton's leader, left his tepee. He was curious about the loud crash he had heard during the night, and he wandered dangerously close to the cliff's edge to see the spectacle. Suddenly he slipped and began to tumble down the steep cliff. He would have perished if it had not been for the branches of a small tree growing a short way down the side of the cliff, which caught him.

Chief White Eagle saw the boy dangling there on the cliff side and responded to the boy's predicament as if it were his own son. He rushed over to his enemy's side on the fallen tree and then reached down to rescue the boy. That day, reconciliation and peace were made between the heads of the two tribes.

In a similar way, God used His Son to bridge the gap between two opposing parties, thereby making us acceptable to Himself. Through Christ, God has made provision for the removal of the contention and animosity that had existed for so long between a holy God and sinful man, establishing peace instead.[6] The two opposing parties had now come into a state of friendship with each other. Jesus has brought us back from estrangement and into harmony with God.[7] Christ has made God's throne of judgment into a place of mercy and grace.

THE BALL'S IN OUR COURT

In summary, this is what happened:

In Eden, God and Adam stood face to face with each other with no barriers between them. When Adam sinned, he turned his back on God, breaking the relationship. Then God used animal sacrifices and ultimately Christ's death to satisfy His demands for sin and offered reconciliation to Adam and his descendants. His Spirit works in us and waits for us to turn around, face God, and accept His terms of restoration.[8]

An unusual true story emerged following World War II. During the war, a Japanese soldier was told by his commanding officer to never surrender to the Americans because they would torture and kill him. At last the war ended, yet this soldier still remained in hiding in the jungles of a Pacific island.

Repeated attempts were made to communicate with him that the war had ceased in 1945. When he finally heard about the war ending, he apparently did not believe it, and so he continued living under miserable conditions when he could have been back with his family, in the comfort and security of his own home. Eventually he did come out of the jungle and surrender—but not until about twenty years later!

It is something like this in the spiritual realm. Christ has made peace possible between God and man by dying in our place. Sadly, many people either have not heard this good news, or they refuse to believe it—and so they continue to live as spiritual fugitives.

Now that God has provided for reconciliation, He entreats us to be reconciled to Him.[9] With outstretched arms, God invites us to come. If, however, we choose to have a hostile attitude toward God and refuse to be reconciled, we will continue to remain God's enemies and under condemnation, with our sins still upon us.[10] For it is **we** who need to be reconciled to God, not God to man.

If we repent of our sins and receive Jesus as ruler over our lives, we will no longer be enemies of God. Instead we will be His children. We will enjoy peace and friendship with God because we will have been reconciled to Him.

If you are living apart from peace and friendship with your heavenly Father, get out of the jungle and come on home! The peace treaty between God and man was signed in the blood of Christ two thousand years ago. Why remain in a state of war with God? Accept peace on His terms.

If you would now like to make your peace *with* God and be reconciled to Him, please turn to page 161 for a prayer to guide you. Then and only then will you have the peace *of* God. As someone once said, "No God, no peace. Know God, know peace."

For if, when we were God's enemies, we were reconciled to Him through the death of His Son, how much more, having been reconciled, shall we be saved through His life! [11]

RECONCILIATION—
A TREASURE FROM THE CROSS

ENDNOTES

1. Romans 5:8-11; Colossians 1:19-23; James 4:4; Ephesians 2:1-3
2. Jeremiah 17:9; Romans 3:9-18, 23
3. 1 John 3:8
4. Isaiah 53:11
5. 1 John 2:2 (KJV); 4:10 (KJV); Romans 3:25 (KJV)
6. Romans 5:1; Isaiah 53:5
7. 1 Peter 3:18
8. Adapted from Henry Clarence Theissen, *Introductory Lectures in Systematic Theology* (Grand Rapids: Wm. B. Eerdmans, 1967), 327.
9. 2 Corinthians 5:18-20
10. John 3:17-18
11. Romans 5:10

MEDICAL INSIGHT INTO THE CRUCIFIXION

As Jesus endured the rigors of His ministry, traveling miles by foot throughout Palestine, many believe that "it is reasonable to assume that [He] was in good physical condition before His walk to Gethsemane. However, during the twelve hours between 9 p.m. Thursday and 9 a.m. Friday, he had suffered great emotional stress…, abandonment by His closest friends…, and a physical beating" after His first trial by the Jews. Add to this "a traumatic and sleepless night, [being] forced to walk more than two-and-a-half miles to and from the trial sites," and lack of food and water, and we see the factors that may have made "Jesus particularly vulnerable to the adverse…effects of the scourging."

Edwards et al., "On the Physical Death of Jesus Christ," 1457.

CHAPTER 5

YOUR SIN DEBT PAID IN FULL:
FORGIVENESS

Pilate called together the chief priests, the rulers and the people, and said to them, "You brought me this man as one who was inciting the people to rebellion. I have examined him in your presence and have found no basis for your charges against him. Neither has Herod, for he sent him back to us; as you can see, he has done nothing to deserve death. Therefore, I will punish him and then release him."

With one voice they cried out, "Away with this man! Release Barabbas to us!"...

Luke 23:13-18

Note: Mark's account of this same event tells us that Pilate knew it was out of envy that the chief priests had handed Jesus over to them (Mark 15:10).

"What shall I do, then, with Jesus who is called Christ?" Pilate asked. They all answered, "Crucify Him!" "Why? What crime has he committed?" asked Pilate.

But they shouted all the louder, "Crucify him!"

When Pilate saw that he was getting nowhere, but that instead an uproar was starting, he took water and washed His hands in front of the crowd. "I am innocent of this man's blood," he said. "It is your responsibility!"

All the people answered, "Let His blood be on us and on our children!" Then he released Barabbas to them. But he had Jesus flogged, and handed him over to be crucified....They stripped him and put a scarlet robe on him, and then wove a crown of thorns and set it on his head.

They put a staff in his right hand and knelt in front of him and mocked him. "Hail, King of the Jews!" they said. They spit on him, and took the staff and struck him on the head again and again. After they had mocked him, they took off the robe and put his own clothes on him. Then they led him away to crucify him.

Matthew 27:22-31

Jesus said, "Father, forgive them, for they do not know what they are doing."

Luke 23:34

I N the greatest travesty of justice, Christ was illegally charged with blasphemy and insurrection by the Jewish religious leaders. He was never proven guilty of these charges but was still sentenced to death. Even after witnessing Christ's awesome miracles—including raising people from the dead—these religious leaders arrested Him, tried Him, and pressured Pilate to give Him the death sentence because of their envy, their power-hungry desire to preserve their leadership positions.[1] These religious leaders were blinded to the truth, and many times we are blinded too because of our own sinful condition.

We are capable of doing the vilest things to others. Have you ever looked back at your life and been shocked at the things you have said and done? Sometimes we do these things because we are convinced that we're doing the right thing; other times it's just because of our own selfish motives. The regret and shame felt later, when we realize how wrong we were, can be overwhelming. But no matter how terrible our sins are or how often they have been committed, we *can* be forgiven by God.[2]

One of the most touching examples of repentance and forgiveness in the Bible is that of a woman in a Galilean village who had a very sinful reputation.[3] Having heard Jesus teach, a transformation must have occurred within her, and it seems that she waited for an opportunity to express her love and gratitude to Him.

One day she learned that He was in the house of Simon, a member of the Pharisees, which was a Jewish religious sect. Boldly, she entered, risking rejection and making her way unnoticed into the dining area, carrying an alabaster flask of fragrant ointment. She approached Jesus and stood at His feet, weeping loudly and uncontrollably.

Sinfulness stood in the presence of Holiness. Would she be rejected and thrown out? She let her tears of repentance and joy fall upon His feet and then wiped His feet dry with her hair. Tenderly and unceasingly, she pressed kisses on those beautiful feet and anointed them with the costly ointment—the feet of the One who had brought to her new life, hope, and forgiveness.

The fact that she had been a notorious sinner did not repulse Jesus as it had Simon—the self-righteous Pharisee who had neglected to wash his guest's dusty feet as was the custom of the day. Having pointed out her example to Simon, Jesus turned to the woman and said, "Your sins are forgiven. Your faith has saved you. Go in peace."

Those whom men condemn can assuredly find mercy and pardon at the feet of Jesus, for He rejects none but receives all who turn to Him in faith and repentance.

Like the woman in the story, we all fall short and sin, despite our best efforts to do what is right.[4] We keep breaking the commandments God gave us in the Bible, even when we don't want to. Therefore, because God's broken laws demand justice, our sin becomes a **debt** that we owe to Him—a legal obligation that we can never repay.[5] It requires eternity in hell.

How Can We Obtain God's Forgiveness?

In our effort to obtain forgiveness of this debt and gain a right standing with God, we often reason that we can do good deeds to earn it. These meritorious "works" include such things as volunteering our time, talent, and resources to worthy causes; charitable giving; water baptism; church attendance and membership; communion, sacraments, ritualistic prayers, and legalistic compliance to the teachings of an ecclesiastical body or to the founder of an organization.

Doing these things may appease our conscience and make us feel good, but it does not get at the heart of the problem. We are still left living in uncertainty, hoping against hope that in the end our good deeds *might* outweigh our bad and entitle us to enter heaven. Unfortunately, it doesn't work that way. Yes, we should be doing good deeds, but doing them to merit forgiveness is giving us a false sense of security.

The logic behind trying to earn forgiveness is wrong on at least two counts:

1. First, our good deeds do not qualify as a means to set us free from our sin debt. They lack the substitutionary requirements already mentioned in the first two chapters of this book. Good deeds are important as acts of obedience to be rewarded. However, they are insufficient and incapable of paying our sin debt and are valueless to merit forgiveness or to earn our way to heaven.

2. Second, God does not weigh our record of good and bad deeds against each other when our life is over. Through Christ, God cancels our sin debt when we receive His forgiveness by faith. Our only hope of being released from the debt of sin that we owe God is through the forgiveness **He** gives.

How, then, can we be forgiven? As we have learned, God always links forgiveness with the shedding of blood of an innocent victim. In fact, the Bible says there can be no forgiveness of sin without the shedding of blood.[6] But whose blood qualifies? Our human blood does not qualify because we are unclean, guilty sinners.

Christ's blood, however, is a different matter.

Jesus was both human and divine—100 percent man and 100 percent God.—and He chose to be the innocent victim for us. Because He was sinless and did not owe a debt of sin Himself, He alone could offer His life and pay the debt of sin we owed. On the cross, Jesus shed His blood for our forgiveness, paying the debt for sin in full—doing for us what we could not do for ourselves.

This means that God has provided for the complete cancellation of the charges that would have convicted us in His court of law.[7] Christ, who will be our Judge,[8] is able to forgive all of our sins and totally clear the record of the debt that we owe. Think of it! The Judge of all the earth came down from off His "bench" and identified with us, the condemned ones, and chose to take our place and pay our penalty Himself!

Through Christ, God has provided for our acquittal. When we trust in Christ's work for us on the cross, God will remove our sins from us, as far as the east is from the west.[9] No longer will any charges be presented to convict us.

FORGIVENESS IS CONDITIONAL

Yet God's bestowal of forgiveness is conditional. It is not automatically given to everyone. First, we must believe that the shedding of Christ's innocent blood is the only remedy for the payment of our debt of sin, and that He is the Son of God who was raised from the dead.

Inseparably intertwined with this faith must be sincere repentance, which means to turn from walking in sin to walking with God instead, in trust and in obedience. This produces fruit in keeping with repentance—like confession of sin to God, restitution, and change of behavior. Jesus Himself said that unless we repented, we would perish.[10] He also taught us that forgiveness from God is dependent on forgiving others who have wronged us.[11]

You see, God isn't primarily interested in apologies. He looks for godly sorrow that results in a different attitude and a change of behavior. In fact, when one genuinely repents, it is proof positive that that person truly has the faith God requires. The act of repentance itself demonstrates a faith so genuine and certain that it manifests itself in a change of thinking and conduct.

A lack of repentance is evidence that one never really had faith in Christ as the Bible defines it. Regardless of what one may say about his or her faith, in the absence of an ongoing character transformation, that "faith" is nothing more than talk—just an intellectual assent. Faith and repentance embody the conversion experience.

GOD PATIENTLY WORKS IN US AND WAITS FOR US

Now that Jesus has completed His work on the cross, He **waits** with great anticipation for us to believe and repent so that He can forgive and pardon us.[12] In fact, God in His kindness is always trying to persistently and patiently bring us to a place of repentance.[13]

A great example of God's patient perseverance in working with us is seen in His dealings with King Manasseh, who reigned over the nation of Judah in Jerusalem 2,600 years ago.[14]

King Manasseh rebelled from serving the true God of his forefathers. Instead he practiced witchcraft, divination, sorcery, and dealt with fortunetellers as well as other demonic occult practices forbidden by God. He rebuilt the pagan sacrificial altars his godly father had torn down, and he instituted religions with "sacred" prostitution and child sacrifice by fire as acts of worship to his heathen gods.

This was not all. Manasseh bowed down and worshipped the sun and moon, and the stars and planets. He repeatedly desecrated the holy temple of God in Jerusalem. He even set up a carved idol of Asherah, the Canaanite goddess of love and fertility, in God's sacred house. He led his whole nation astray and caused them to grossly sin, and he filled Jerusalem with much innocent blood. The Bible describes no one more wicked than he!

Yet God dealt with Manasseh with great mercy and long-suffering. God sent His prophets to speak to him, but he turned a deaf ear. Finally God had to send the Assyrian army against Manasseh, and they captured him and put hooks in his nose, binding him with chains and leading him a prisoner to their land. Through this terrible affliction, God was able to get through to him and reveal Himself. In his distress, Manasseh greatly humbled himself before the true God and entreated Him through prayer.

Amazingly, God was so moved by Manasseh's genuine faith and repentance that He forgave him of all his wickedness and miraculously restored his kingdom back to him in Jerusalem. Acting in the fear of God, Manasseh now demonstrated true repentance as he removed the false gods that he had set up. In their place, he restored the altar of the true God with its sacrifices in the temple. He even ordered his nation to serve the true God alone.

The Holy Spirit is still convicting us of sin today. How remarkable that God would love us so much that He would patiently and graciously seek after us to try to bring us into right relationship with Him. When we respond, Jesus said that *"there is rejoicing in the presence of the angels of God over one sinner who repents."*[15] He is trying to get through to you today!

If you are someone who just cannot forgive yourself for something bad you have done, there is great news for you! Consider King Manasseh! Are you a worse sinner than he? God enabled him to forgive himself for all the terrible evil he had done.

God does not want you to carry around that heavy load of guilt and shame. He wants to lift it from you and carry it far, far away so that you can be free of its weight. So if God hasn't given up on you and is more than willing to forgive you when you repent, how can **you** not forgive yourself? He wants so much to exchange the guilt and shame you bear with His peace and to cleanse you from your sins.

FORGIVENESS AND CONSEQUENCES

However, it is important to remember that there will be natural consequences for our sinful deeds, which will continue to take effect even after we have repented and God has forgiven us (i.e., probation or jail time, health problems, loss of public trust). [16] This is due to God's law of planting and harvesting.[17] But God can help us use these mistakes and failures as learning tools, ultimately molding us more and more into the image of Christ. God has even promised to masterfully use those painful consequences in our lives to help us grow in Him and to turn them around for our good when we love Him.[18]

When others remind us of the details of our dreadful sins, or when we have to live through the difficult consequences of the wrong we have done, we must rest in the fact that, when we repented, God forgave us and cancelled the debt of sin that we owed.

OUR SINS ARE FORGOTTEN BY GOD

Like the files that are erased when we press the delete key on a computer keyboard, our sins are forgotten by God when we repent, never to be held against us again.[19] Either God does not remember them because our record of sins disappears as if they were never committed, or else the charges are cancelled and beside each sin are stamped the words "Debt paid in full" because of our wonderful Christ! I think the latter.

Because Jesus paid our debt of sin, sin loses its power to convict us and to bring us under God's penalty. And just as senseless as it is to try and hack into a computer's hard drive to find those deleted files that are no longer needed, so too is it ridiculous for us to try to dig up past sins that God has already forgiven, forgotten, and removed from our account.

OUR ONGOING NEED FOR FORGIVENESS

Now what about our ongoing need for forgiveness and cleansing in the future? God gave us a wonderful illustration right in our own bodies. If we look at the operation of our kidneys, we will see an illustration of how the continuous forgiveness and cleansing of our sins occur through the blood of Jesus.

Impurities and poisons in our bloodstream are carried by our arteries to the kidneys, which filter them out. As a result, pure, clean blood flows out from the kidneys and is carried back by the veins to provide life to the cells in our bodies. In the same way, as we bring our sins to

Jesus, He takes the impurities and poisons of our sins and continuously cleanses us from all sin—giving us life and health. If we have to go to God for this today, we can still go to Him again tomorrow!

You may be asking, "Could these things really be true?" Don't doubt it for a second. It is part of the good news that Christ purchased for us on that terrible cross. God promises, *"If we confess our sins, he is faithful and just and will forgive us our sins and purify us from all unrighteousness."*[20]

If you have not yet received the forgiveness that Christ offers you, won't you receive it right now? Turn to page 161 for a prayer to guide you.

FORGIVENESS—
A TREASURE FROM THE CROSS

ENDNOTES

1. Mark 15:6-11; John 11:43-48
2. Matthew 12:31-32
3. Luke 7:36-50
4. Romans 3:23
5. Matthew 18:21-35; 6:12; Romans 4:4
6. Hebrews 9:22; Matthew 26:28
7. Colossians 2:13-14
8. John 5:22, 27, 30; Acts 10:38-42
9. Psalm 103:8-12
10. Luke 13:1-5; Acts 2:37-38; Proverbs 28:13
11. Matthew 6:14-15; 18:21-35; Luke 17:3-4; Colossians 3:13; Ephesians 4:32

12. Isaiah 55:6-7; Acts 3:19
13. Romans 2:4
14. 2 Chronicles 33:1-19
15. Luke 15:3-10; 2 Peter 3:9
16. 2 Samuel 11:1-12:14; 13:1-39; 16:20-23
17. Galatians 6:7-8
18. Romans 8:28
19. Isaiah 43:25; 38:17; Jeremiah 31:34; Micah 7:18-19; Hebrews 8:12
20. 1 John 1:9

MEDICAL INSIGHT INTO THE CRUCIFIXION

"Flogging was a legal preliminary to every Roman execution, and only women and Roman senators or soldiers (except...for desertion) were exempt." Scourging "was intended to weaken the victim to a state just short of collapse or death."

A short whip called a flagrum was generally used. It had "several single or braided leather thongs of variable lengths, in which small iron balls or sharp pieces of sheep bones were tied at intervals."

The victim "was stripped of his clothing, and his hands were tied to an upright post. The back, buttocks and legs were flogged by two soldiers (called lictors) or by one who alternated positions. The severity of the scourging depended on [their] disposition....As the Roman soldiers repeatedly struck the victim's back with full force, the iron balls would cause deep contusions, and the leather thongs and sheep bones would cut into the skin and subcutaneous tissues. Then as the flogging continued, the lacerations would tear [deeper] into the underlying skeletal muscles and produce quivering ribbons of bleeding flesh."

"It is not known whether the number of lashes [Jesus received] was limited to 39, in accordance with Jewish law" or if it fell under Roman law. "At the Praetorium, Jesus was severely whipped [as] implied in... 1 Peter 2:24. A detailed word study of the ancient Greek text for this verse indicates that the scourging of Jesus was particularly harsh And remember, "hematidrosis had rendered his skin particularly tender." Agonizing pain and considerable "blood loss generally set the stage for circulatory shock. The extent of blood loss may well have determined how long the victim would survive on the cross."

Edwards et al., "On the Physical Death of Jesus Christ," 1457-1458, 1461.

CHAPTER 6

DECLARED "NOT GUILTY":
JUSTIFICATION

*Two other men, both criminals, were also led out with him
to be executed. When they came to the place called The Skull,
there they crucified him, along with the criminals—one on
his right, the other on his left....One of the criminals who
hung there hurled insults at him: "Aren't you the Christ? Save
yourself and us!"*

*But the other criminal rebuked him. "Don't you fear God," he
said, "since you are under the same sentence? We are pun-
ished justly, for we are getting what our deeds deserve. But
this man has done nothing wrong."*

*Then he said, "Jesus, remember me when you come into your
kingdom." Jesus answered him, "I tell you the truth, today
you will be with me in paradise."*

Luke 23:32-33, 39-43

TWO crosses. One is a cross of rejection. The other is a cross of
reception. These two crosses depict God's gift of free will—He
will respect our decisions, even if they are wrong.

The first thief wanted to be physically rescued from his situation. In
his mind, if Jesus couldn't keep him from dying, then he had no use for

Him! The second thief, however, was penitent. He knew he was going to die and called out to Christ for mercy in eternity. Christ's response was, *"Today you will be with me in paradise."*

Dying there on the cross, this thief was unable to move his hands or feet to perform any righteous deeds or sacraments—unable to express the intent of his heart through actions. If justification had to be earned by good works, this thief certainly could not have entered into paradise with Jesus.

Each of us will identify with one or the other of these two thieves crucified with Jesus. One rejected Christ, died with his sins still upon him, and went to unending torment in hell. The other thief received Christ, died with his sins taken from him, and went to eternal joy in heaven.

The Holy Spirit gave us this true story to show that we can only get to heaven by faith in Christ's work on the cross—not because of anything we do to earn or merit it, not even in part.

We see in this real-life account that the basis for entering into heaven is apart from any good deeds. Our justification must be received as a **gift** of God's mercy and grace, His unmerited favor—or else we can't have it at all. A gift cannot be earned. It has to be accepted and received—or else rejected.

The Bible says that the person who trusts in Christ's work for himself as the basis of being justified, this person's **faith** is counted as righteousness. How? Through what the Bible calls *imputation*. Imputation means, "to put to one's account." God the Father *imputes* the righteousness of Christ's sinless life to our spiritual bank account.[1]

ENVISION YOURSELF BEFORE GOD'S COURT OF JUSTICE

Now, picture a courtroom scene in heaven. Let's say that today you are not right with God and are facing His judgment. The moment you repent and receive His Son by **faith** as the substitute for your sins, God gives you a new status with Him. He declares you "not guilty" and places you, a sinner, in the position of a righteous person. You are given a right standing with God. This is called justification.[2]

Whether you feel justified or not has little to do with your actually being justified in God's sight. The courtroom terminology is meant to show us that our justification becomes a matter of legal record in God's eyes—it is a fact to be accepted by faith.

Justification does not **make** you righteous; it **declares** you righteous. God forgives your sins and treats you **just as if you had never sinned**.

Now when God looks at you, all He sees is Christ's righteousness draped over your sins.

Once we are declared righteous, our righteous standing will not be any greater today, or tomorrow, or at any point in the future than it was the day we gave our lives to Christ. God justifies us as a one-time transaction. There is nothing we can do to add to Christ's work on the cross, such as accumulating good works throughout our lifetime, to somehow make ourselves "more justified." We are completely justified through Christ, and it is impossible to become any more justified.

Once we receive the gift of Christ's work for us, true faith in Him should result in obedience to God's will and produce good works as its natural fruit.[3] These "good works" we do in Christ's name will be rewarded someday—but they can never earn us a right standing before God. As the words of the old hymn *Rock of Ages* say, "Nothing in my hands I bring, simply to Thy cross I cling."[4]

Christ's sacrifice is what makes our justification possible.[5] The two parts of the cross symbolize this. The vertical beam of the cross represents the height of God's holiness, which we sinners cannot attain. The horizontal beam represents the endless expanse of God's love that reaches out to us all. The crucifixion of His Son on these beams as our substitute enables God to forgive us without lowering His standards, to mercifully impute Christ's righteousness to us while still remaining just.[6]

JUSTIFICATION ILLUSTRATED

Perhaps the best illustration of justification is that of a lunar eclipse. Just as the sun shines on the earth so that the moon is completely covered by the earth's shadow, in a similar way God the Father looks at you through His Son Jesus and sees you completely covered with His righteousness. He does not see you; He sees Christ. God pronounces you "not guilty" and gives you a new legal standing. In this way, like the penitent thief, you become justified, or made right, in God's sight!

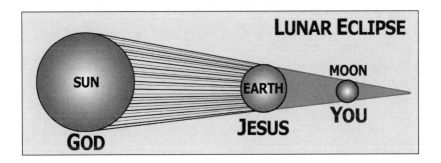

JUSTIFICATION—
A TREASURE FROM THE CROSS

ENDNOTES

1. Romans 4:1-25; 3:20-24, 28-30; Galatians 3:6-11

2. Galatians 2:15-16; Philippians 3:9

3. Ephesians 2:8-10; Titus 3:5-8; Colossians 1:10; Luke 3:8; John 15:1-8, 14-17; Matthew 7:17-20

4. *Rock of Ages* by Augustus M. Toplady, 1775

5. Isaiah 53:11-12; Acts 13:38-39; Romans 4:25; 5:1, 9

6. Adapted from *He Chose the Nails: What God Did to Win Your Heart* by Max Lucado. ©2000 Max Lucado. Word Publishing, Nashville, TN.

HISTORICAL INSIGHT INTO THE CRUCIFIXION

Crucifixion is one of the most humiliating, horrific, tortuous, and painful deaths ever conceived. It "probably first began among the Persians. Alexander the Great introduced the practice to Egypt and Carthage, and the Romans appear to have learned of it from the Carthaginians." The Romans then "perfected [crucifixion] as a form of torture and capital punishment that was designed to produce a slow death with maximum pain and suffering."

"It was one of the most disgraceful and cruel methods of execution, and usually was reserved only for slaves, foreigners, revolutionaries, and the vilest of criminals. Roman law usually protected Roman citizens from it except perhaps in the case of desertion by soldiers....Death by crucifixion, was in every sense of the word, excruciating (Latin, *excruciatus*, or 'out of the cross')."

Edwards et al., "On the Physical Death of Jesus Christ," 1458, 1461.

CHAPTER 7

WHOLENESS FOR SPIRIT, SOUL, AND BODY:
HEALING

When Jesus' followers saw what was going to happen...one of them struck the servant of the high priest, cutting off his right ear. But Jesus answered, "No more of this!" And he touched the man's ear and healed him.

Luke 22:49-51

The Sovereign Lord has opened my ears, and I have not been rebellious; I have not drawn back. I offered my back to those who beat me, my cheeks to those who pulled out my beard; I did not hide my face from mocking and spitting.

Isaiah 50:5-6

He had no beauty or majesty to attract us to him, nothing in his appearance that we should desire him. He was despised and rejected by men, a man of sorrows, and familiar with suffering. Like one from whom men hide their faces he was despised, and we esteemed him not.

But he was pierced for our transgressions, he was crushed for our iniquities; the punishment that brought us peace was upon him, and by his wounds we are healed.

Isaiah 53:2-5

HOW ironic it was that before His hands were bound, the last thing Jesus did was to miraculously heal someone.

Because man is a unity of spirit, soul, and body,[1] his whole being was affected by sin through Adam's fall in the garden. Though God never intended sickness and suffering, these came directly into the human race as a result of the Fall and its subsequent curse on mankind. Sin introduced disease, infirmity, and brokenness into our world. A sin-diseased couple propagated a sin-diseased race.

So when Jesus was crucified for the sins of the human race, His death was intended to save and to heal the whole man. Jesus not only took our sins upon Himself, but He bore our sicknesses and diseases too.[2] He did this not just to experience our sufferings but to save, to heal, and to deliver us from them.

Jesus provided for healing in your spirit, body, mind, and emotions. He took the infirmities of a hurting world and bore the full weight of them upon Himself, as if they were His own, so that you could be relieved and freed from them.

GOD STILL HEALS TODAY

During His earthly ministry, no sickness was beyond His power. Jesus constantly reached out and healed hurting people who believed in Him.[3] Christ is still the same today. He has not changed. He has come to heal the brokenhearted, the broken in body, the broken in spirit. Having experienced life as we do on this earth, Jesus fully knows what we are going through, and He is still healing people through the power of the Holy Spirit. There have been many documented evidences of this, right up through today.

Clearly then we should seek healing wholeheartedly, persistently laying hold of it by faith in God's character and promise. Healing is biblical, and God miraculously heals people today—some instantaneously and some through progressive recovery.

In fact, among the supernatural gifts that God has given to the body of Christ are the *"gifts of healing."*[4] The same third person of the Trinity who worked these miracles in the Old Testament, through Jesus while He was here on earth, through the twelve apostles, and through countless others throughout this church age will continue to do so today and into the future.[5]

HOW DOES HEALING OCCUR?

Healing comes in various ways, but especially as the human agent obeys the Holy Spirit's direction. Sometimes a person is prompted to say a word authoritatively to the afflicted and healing then takes place.[6] On other occasions the healing takes place by the laying on of hands,[7] by anointing with oil,[8] or on rare occasions through objects that are prayed over and taken to the sick to increase their faith.[9] At still other times we must contend in prayer against evil spirits before healing occurs.[10]

Sometimes conditions have to be met by the sick, and as they obey they are made whole.[11] Then there are instances when a believer is led by the Spirit to pray and physically touch the sick in some way.[12] Some are healed by their own faith in God's character and promises while others are healed through the faith of the one praying. There is no set formula for healing. God heals in many types of ways.

WHY SOME PEOPLE ARE NOT HEALED

We will never fully understand why some are not healed in this lifetime. There are many possible reasons.[13] For one thing, God did not promise that we as Christians would be exempt from suffering. He did, however, promise that if we love Him, He would always be with us through every circumstance of life and would bring something good out of every situation.

The famous hymn writer, Fanny Crosby, was blinded when she was only six weeks old by an improper medical treatment, and she was never healed. Yet she did not consider blindness a handicap; she counted it as a blessing. At age thirty she had a dramatic conversion experience, and when she was thirty-eight, she married a blind musician and teacher. At age forty-five, endowed by God with incredible musical and poetry-writing abilities, she wrote her first gospel hymn—just shortly after losing her baby, who died in early infancy. It is estimated that during her ninety-five years of life, Fanny Crosby wrote over eight thousand hymn texts—more than any other known hymn writer.[14] She left us the priceless gifts of her songs, which have brought countless people closer to Christ. Without her afflictions and misfortunes, perhaps none of these songs ever would have been written.

It all boils down to our view of God and whether we can trust Him completely with our lives. Is your God fallible or infallible? Does He have flaws, or is He flawless? Can He make mistakes, or is He perfect? Some people lose faith in God and quit serving Him because they cannot reconcile a God who allows evil and suffering or seemingly won't heal a loved one. We can put our trust in the God of the Bible who has no flaws or limitations and always has our very best at heart...or we can choose to be bitter, falsely believing that He is not concerned or has overlooked and forgotten us.

GOD IS INTIMATELY INVOLVED IN YOUR LIFE

The Bible teaches us that God is involved in everything that affects the life of a child of God—even those things that we bring on ourselves.[15] What I mean by this is that everything that happens is either **sent** by Him, **permitted** by Him, or **used** by Him. By "bring it on yourself," I'm referring to the law of planting and harvesting, whereby we make wrong decisions and must live with the consequences.[16] And even in these instances, God will use our failures to advance His purposes in our lives if we but love and trust Him.

Many times we are like the young boy who was playing with his toys one evening on the living room floor. His mother was sitting on the couch above him, doing needlepoint. At some point, the boy looked up and remarked, "Ma, whatever you're making doesn't look so good down here. It doesn't make sense."

Surprised, she flipped over the frame to show him the beautiful pattern she was stitching. "What do you mean, dear?" she asked him. "Don't you like my butterfly?" As the boy saw the topside of the needlepoint, he realized that it really was beautiful, that he just had to look at it from the right perspective to see it for what it really was.

Like that boy, many times we think our lives don't make sense. From our earthly perspective, we only see a distorted, unfinished jumble of threads instead of the wonderful tapestry that our infinitely wise heavenly Father is weaving in our lives, for our ultimate good and His glory.

We know that our bodies are decaying daily and are in the process of dying. It will only be on the great Day of Resurrection that our bodies will see total healing and redemption—never to feel pain or be ill again.[17] As believers, we have this certain hope, that someday we will be healed completely and for eternity—with perfect new bodies created for an everlasting existence with God.

Truly Christ has carried away our sorrows and griefs, our weaknesses and pains, our sicknesses and bodily diseases. The Bible declares that *"by His wounds you have been healed."*[18] We can be fully delivered and made whole. Christ has **already** provided for our healing today, for our spirit, soul, and body. Reach out. Lay claim to it and take hold of it by faith in His promise.

In the meantime, as you go through your trial, allow God to do a rich work in your heart and life as you patiently wait for His deliverance. Remember that when you are distressed, God is also distressed.[19] If you should feel that God has forgotten you in your affliction, take comfort in what God says to you in His holy Word: *"Can a mother forget the baby at her breast and have no compassion on the child she has borne? Though she may forget, I will not forget you! See, I have engraved you on the palms of my hands."*[20]

HEALING—
A TREASURE FROM THE CROSS

ENDNOTES

1. 1 Thessalonians 5:23; Hebrews 4:12
2. Isaiah 53:4-5
3. Matthew 4:23-24; 8:16-17; 9:35; 15:29-31; Luke 5:17; 6:17-19
4. 1 Corinthians 12:9, 28
5. John 14:11-12; 16:7-13; Acts 10:38; Matthew 10:1; Mark 16:17-18
6. Matthew 12:9-13
7. Mark 6:5
8. Mark 6:13; James 5:14-16
9. Acts 19:11-12
10. Luke 13:10-13
11. Luke 17:11-14; 2 Kings 5:1, 10-14
12. Matthew 8:1-3; 9:27-30
13. Numbers 14:18; 2 Kings 5:16-27; Psalm 119:67, 71, 75; Job 2:1-10; Luke 13:10-16; Matthew 13:58; John 5:14-15, 9:1-3; 2 Corinthians 1:3-7; Hebrews 2:9-10, 18; 5: 8; 2 Corinthians 12:7-10; 1 Peter 4:1-2, 12-13, 19
14. Kenneth Osbeck, *101 More Hymn Stories* (Kregel Publications,Grand Rapids, Michigan, 1985), 237-241.
15. Romans 8:28
16. Galatians 6:7-8
17. Romans 8:22-24; 1 Corinthians 15:50-53
18. 1 Peter 2:24; Exodus 15:26; Psalm 103:1-3; 147:3
19. Isaiah 63:9
20. Isaiah 49:14-16; Matthew 10:29-30

HISTORICAL INSIGHT INTO THE CRUCIFIXION

The cross consisted of an upright wooden post (*stipes*) that weighed approximately 200 pounds and a horizontal crossbar (*patibulum*) weighing 75 to 125 pounds. The *stipes* was permanently located in the ground at the crucifixion site outside the city walls.

"It was customary for the condemned man to carry his own cross from the flogging post to the site of crucifixion [where the stipes was located]....He was usually naked, unless this was prohibited by local customs. The *patibulum*...was placed across the nape of the victim's neck and balanced along both shoulders [which were already painfully lacerated from the scourging]. Usually, the outstretched arms then were tied to the crossbar."

A complete Roman military guard, headed by a centurion, led the processional to the site of the crucifixion. "Jesus apparently was so weakened by the severe flogging that he could not carry the patibulum from the Praetorium to the site of crucifixion one third of a mile away.... Therefore, even before the actual crucifixion, Jesus' physical condition was at least serious and possibly critical."

Edwards et al., "On the Physical Death of Jesus Christ," 1458-1459, 1461.

CHAPTER 8

BECOMING A MEMBER OF GOD'S FAMILY:
ADOPTION

Near the cross of Jesus stood his mother, his mother's sister,
Mary the wife of Clopas, and Mary of Magdala. When Jesus
saw his mother there, and the disciple whom he loved stand-
ing nearby, he said to his mother, "Dear woman, here is your
son," and to the disciple, "Here is your mother." From that
time on, this disciple took her into his home.

John 19:25-27

IN the midst of His own great agony on the cross, Jesus had concern for the care of others. From this account we assume that Christ's earthly father Joseph was no longer living. Jesus entrusted the care of His mother to John, His closest friend and disciple. John would continue to protect and provide for Mary.

Families are so important. We all recognize the value of being raised in a good family. The genes we inherit, the love and quality of care we receive, and the shaping of our character and values are all results of the type of family to which we belong.

How true this is in the spiritual realm, especially with regard to God's family! Yet it may come as a surprise that although God is everyone's Creator, He is not everyone's Father. That relationship is only possible through adoption.

LIVING IN THE DEVIL'S DOMAIN

You see, when Adam was originally created in the image of God, God called His creation *"very good,"* and Adam was in fact called a *"son"* of God.[1] One of God's designs in creating Adam was that he and his descendants would have dominion over the earth.[2] However, when Satan, an evil fallen angel, tempted Adam and Eve in the Garden of Eden, they chose to disobey God.

Through their act of rebellion, they chose to serve themselves (and Satan) rather than God. Sin entered the human race and gave the devil control over mankind. As a result—it may shock you to realize this— every single person is born as a subject into Satan's kingdom.[3]

Adam's nature no longer wholly reflected the character of God. To a large extent, it now mirrored Satan's character, which is wholly opposed to the nature of God. As a result, the fallen nature of Adam's descendants is so unlike God's nature that Jesus referred to fallen man as *"children of the wicked one."*[4] This is because Adam and Eve had acted like and served Satan, which caused all of their descendants to become children of the devil.[5]

Thank God this awful, tragic story does not end here. Jesus made it possible for us to be adopted back into the perfect loving care of His heavenly Father. Now, instead of staying under Satan's control, we may choose to leave his kingdom and enter God's kingdom.

Compare Two Fathers

Let us take a minute to compare the character of God with that of Satan. In doing this, we will see clearly how differently each father treats his children.[6] And let us always remember God's infinite superiority over Satan in every way. Though powerful and intelligent, Satan is merely an angel—and a fallen one at that.[7]

First of all, God loves you; Satan hates you. God will always be faithful and will never leave or forsake you; Satan will be unfaithful and desert you. God will reveal the truth and remove your blindness; Satan will deceive you and lead you to believe a lie. God will guide you into paths that will save you; Satan will set a trap to destroy you.

God sets you free, but Satan enslaves you. God will always show you compassion, but Satan shows no mercy. God will forgive and defend you, but Satan slanders and accuses you. God will provide for your needs and give you everything richly to be enjoyed, but Satan robs you and makes you destitute.

God will give you His wealth for eternity; Satan can only make you rich for a season. God will use you and reward you, both now and in eternity; Satan will use you and drop you once his purposes are met. God gives comfort, support, and hope; Satan causes torment, discouragement, and despair. God will help you bear your burdens and lift them from you; Satan will pile on more and more burdens to crush you. God wants to take you to be with Him in the eternal joys of heaven; Satan wants to take you with him to eternal destruction in the lake of fire.

THE BENEFITS OF ADOPTION

Thankfully, we no longer have to live as children under Satan's oppressive hand. We can become children of God! Think of it: What an awesome reality! We enter God's family through a *"born again"* experience, and then through adoption we enjoy the infinite loving care of our heavenly Father.[8]

What does being *"born again"* mean? The Bible says you were dead in your relationship with God due to sin.[9] When you invite Christ into your heart, the Holy Spirit literally comes into your being.[10] Your spirit comes alive in its relationship with God because it has been regenerated, which is the impartation of God's life and divine character.[11] You become a *"new creation."*[12]

When you are truly born again, there is nothing you can do to become more of a child of God than you already are—although you and I will determine how close and committed our relationship with Christ will be.[13]

In this way, God takes the broken mess of our lives and makes something beautiful out of them.

During the Great Depression, a renowned artist named Henry visited an old high school buddy, Zach, at his villa in the mountains. Henry lodged in the spacious third-floor guest room.

The suite had expensive antique furniture and was decorative and elegant with one exception. One of the walls had a large rusty water stain over most of it, caused by an old leak in the roof. Zach had tried to cover it with the best paint available at the time, but no matter what he did, the stain kept bleeding through.

After a few days, Henry and Zach's refreshing visit came to an end, and the two friends parted, embracing each other as they bid farewell.

The next day, Zach's maid returned from her week of vacation. Near noontime she asked her boss to please come upstairs. She led him into the guest room, where, to his surprise and delight, Zach found that Henry had left him a very memorable gift. Henry had transformed that disfigured, stained wall, painting on it a beautiful flowing waterfall bordered by trees—perfectly capturing the mountainous terrain that surrounded the villa.

This illustration just scratches the surface of what God does with us when He masterfully transforms the stain of sin in our lives into beauty. From the moment we repent and choose to receive Jesus as Savior and ruler over our lives, God makes us His children and adopts us into His family.

The biblical meaning of the term *adoption* goes beyond just being a member of God's family; it includes bestowing adult status as an heir, with full inheritance rights being granted to someone who did not naturally hold those rights.

Through this act of adoption, God the Father gives us a new position—the privilege of sonship,[14] outranking even the angels![15] In being placed in the position of sons, we are beneficiaries, receiving all the privileges of the inheritance that accompanies that sonship.

The Father graciously gives us His Holy Spirit as the down payment for our inheritance, letting us know that He is serious about His intentions toward us, guaranteeing everything else He has promised.[16]

Now let's look at what else happens when God transfers us into His kingdom. The Holy Spirit baptizes the believer into the church, the body of Christ, which is comprised of all truly *"born again"* believers, from every Christian denomination and fellowship worldwide. This awesome privilege allows us to have fellowship with our other adopted brothers and sisters in Christ—a body of believers who are called to give sacrificial love and care to one another.[17]

Jesus left the wealth and glories of heaven and laid aside His divine rights to come to us on this earth.[18] He became poor that we might become spiritually rich![19] If we become adopted sons, we become heirs of God and coheirs with Christ, for as we share in His sufferings, we will also share in the great riches and glory that Jesus receives from His Father.[20] For *"no eye has seen, no ear has heard, no mind has conceived what God has prepared for those who love him."*[21]

HOW TO BECOME ADOPTED

Have you been adopted into God's family yet? Knowing all that He has in store for you as a member of His family, how could you refuse to respond to His invitation? There is a prayer on page 161 that can help you start the process of being adopted into the family of God.

The relationships and rewards you will experience as a child of God are far beyond anything you could ever imagine. But the consequences you will know if you remain a child of Satan are infinitely more painful than the very worst pain you've ever known on earth. If you haven't already done so, won't you leave Satan's kingdom and make the choice to be adopted into God's family today?

ADOPTION—
A TREASURE FROM THE CROSS

ENDNOTES

1. Genesis 1:31; Luke 3:38
2. Genesis 1:26
3. Matthew 12:26; Ephesians 2:1-2; 6:10-12; 1 John 5:19; Luke 4:5-7
4. Matthew 13:38 (KJV)
5. 1 John 3:8-12; John 8:42-44
6. Luke 8:26-30; 13:11; Mark 9:14-27
7. Isaiah 14:12-15; Ezekiel 28:11-19
8. John 1:12-13; 3:3; Ephesians 1:3-6
9. Ephesians 2:1-5; Colossians 2:13
10. 1 Corinthians 6:19
11. 2 Peter 1:4; Titus 3:4-5
12. 2 Corinthians 5:17
13. Luke 9:28-29; Matthew 26:36-37; James 2:23; Hebrews 12:5-11; Revelation 21:7;
14. Romans 8:14-17; Galatians 4:4-7
15. 1 Corinthians 6:3
16. Ephesians 1:13-14
17. 1 Corinthians 12:13-27
18. Philippians 2:5-11
19. 2 Corinthians 8:9
20 Romans 8:17-23
21. 1 Corinthians 2:9 (NIV)

"At the site of execution, by law, the victim was given a bitter drink of wine mixed with myrrh (gall) as a mild analgesic [Author's note: This was done to numb the senses, but Christ refused to be drugged to escape the pain.]...and was then thrown to the ground on his back, with his arms outstretched along the patibulum...in preparation for transfixion of the hands. His wounds from scourging most likely would be torn open again and contaminated with dirt."

"With arms outstretched but not taut, the wrists were nailed to the crossbar. It has been shown that the ligaments and bones of the wrist can support the weight of a body hanging from them, but the palms cannot....The driven nail, [though not fracturing any bones], would crush or sever the rather large sensorimotor median nerve...producing excruciating bolts of fiery pain in both arms...and result in paralysis of a portion of the hand....After both arms were fixed to the crossbar, it and the victim together were lifted onto the stipes."

Next, the feet were usually nailed directly to the front of the stipes with the knees bent. Ropes were also used, but nailing apparently was the preferred Roman practice. "It is likely that the deep peroneal nerve and branches of the medial and lateral plantar nerves would have been injured by the nails."

"The archaeological remains of a crucified body, found in an ossuary near Jerusalem and dating from the time of Christ, indicate that the nails were tapered iron spikes approximately 5 to 7 inches long with a square shaft 3/8 inches across."

"To prolong the crucifixion process, a horizontal wooden block serving as a crude seat (sedile or sedulum) often was attached midway down the stipes [to make breathing easier]."

Unlike scourging, which caused considerable blood loss, "crucifixion per se was a relatively bloodless procedure since no major arteries, other than perhaps the deep plantar arch, pass through [the normal points where the nails were driven]."[1]

Furthermore, Metherall believes that the massive strain on the wrists, arms and shoulders resulted in a dislocation of the shoulder and elbow joints (see Psalm 22:14).[2]

---

1. Edwards et al., "On the Physical Death of Jesus Christ," 1459-1461.
2. A. Metherall, "Christ's Physical Suffering," Firefighters for Christ, Westminister, CA.

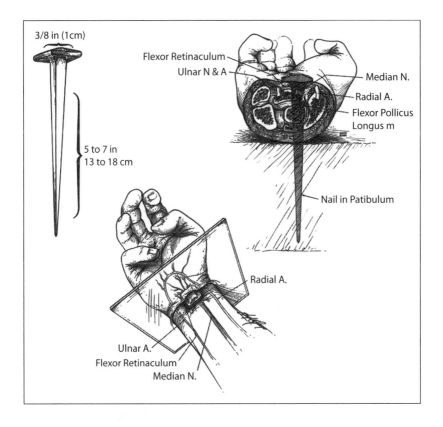

3/8 in (1cm)

Flexor Retinaculum
Ulnar N & A
Median N.
Radial A.
Flexor Pollicus
Longus m

5 to 7 in
13 to 18 cm

Nail in Patibulum

Radial A.

Ulnar A.
Flexor Retinaculum
Median N.

Nailing of wrists. *Left*, Size of iron nail. *Center*, Location of nail in wrist, between carpals and radius. *Right*, Cross section of wrist, at level of plane indicated at left, showing path of nail, with probable transection of median nerve and impalement of flexor pollicis longus, but without injury to major arterial trunks and without fractures of bones.

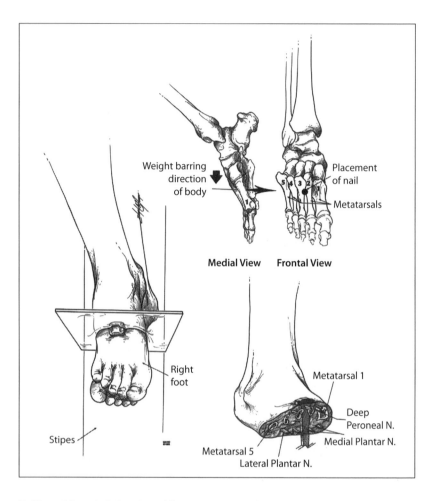

Nailing of feet. *Left*, Position of feet atop one another and against stipes. *Upper right*, Location of nail in second intermetatarsal space. *Lower right*, Cross section of foot, at plane indicated at left, showing path of nail.

CHAPTER 9

PURCHASED BY GOD:
Redemption

With your blood you purchased men for God from every tribe and language and people and nation.

Revelation 5:9

For he has rescued us from the dominion of darkness and brought us into the kingdom of the Son he loves, in whom we have redemption.

Colossians 1:13-14

The son of man did not come to be served, but to serve, and to give his life as a ransom for many.

Matthew 20:28

W HEN used in the New Testament, the word *redemption* means the payment of a price to either buy back a person who is enslaved or to free someone facing a penalty.

Spiritually we need redemption because, according to the Bible, we are born into this world as slaves to both sin[1] and Satan[2] and we are under God's justifiable death penalty.

Christ redeemed us in three main ways:

1. He rescued us from being held as captives to Satan—thereby recovering His rightful ownership of us.
2. He liberated us from sin's enslaving power over our lives.
3. He freed us from the death penalty called for in the Old Testament legal system.

RESCUING US AS CAPTIVES

Let us try to portray this aspect of redemption through a story about John and Carol, a married couple who desperately wanted to have a child. After many years of trying to have children and suffering two disappointing and painful miscarriages, finally their long-awaited dream came true. It was a baby girl, and her parents named her Sara. At once, Sara became the very center of their lives and affection.

One day, when Sara was older and in grade school, tragedy struck. Her mother died, leaving John to be the sole provider for his only child. He did his very best to love and nurture her, but when Sara reached her midteens she began to hang out with the wrong crowd and became increasingly rebellious.

One warm spring day she ran away from home. John immediately reported her missing to the police. Desperately, he inquired of them as to her whereabouts. Eventually he learned that she had been abducted and smuggled to a foreign country that trafficked in the child slave trade. Contacting the embassy in that country, he was told they did not know where she was and did not have the resources to track her down, but they would do the very best they could working with the local authorities.

Upon hearing this disappointing news, John's heart sank, and a cold, numb, empty feeling washed over him. Because he deeply loved Sara and felt responsible for her well-being, he knew that he could not just sit idly by and wait for others to act. Something had to be done immediately.

John devised a bold plan to find and rescue Sara at the risk of his life. He would travel to this poor foreign country and do whatever it took to get his child back—no matter what the cost. This plan was daring and dangerous, but he believed he had no other choice.

First he learned the language and customs of the nation. Then he flew to their country where he grew a beard and worked hard to blend in among them, even dressing as they did. One day he got a break in the case and was ecstatic to learn that Sara might be alive, and even the place where she could be located! He immediately traveled to the town where he heard that Sara might be. While there, he soon learned that some children were to be sold clandestinely in an old vacant warehouse. He found out where the place was, and with anxious heart he went.

When the children were brought out, he couldn't believe his eyes. There she was! The children were to be auctioned off to the highest bidders, and Sara happened to be one of them! As he gazed intently at her, her body looked frail and her will and spirit broken He wondered with anguish what they had done to her.

He was so close to getting her back—yet so far away. Believing it could be dangerous to expose who he really was, he thought it best to continue to hide his true identity. Finally his daughter's turn came. Bidding for his daughter began as a short, ill-tempered man searching for a bargain made the first bid. A wealthy lady who owned a local brothel countered his. Speaking in their language, Sara's father made the next offer, followed by a calculating merchant who traded regularly for slaves, looking for cheap labor. Frightened, the girl stood there staring down at her chained hands and feet.

Finally, unbeknownst to Sara, it was her father who made the highest bid! As they led the girl to her new owner, fear and anxiety welled up within her as she wondered what this new master would do with her. Without saying a word and being careful to remain anonymous, her father led her away quietly to a secluded spot. Then lifting his daughter's downcast face and looking into her eyes, he said, "Sara, it's me!"

At that moment, when she heard her name, she remembered the voice. "Father!"

As he embraced his daughter, he whispered, "Sara, you're free." With utter amazement, she stood trembling and crying, as he unchained her hands and feet. "Thank you, Daddy; thank you," Sara cried with joy as she fell at his feet. "What can I ever do to repay you? You traveled all the way over here and risked your life to rescue me."

They quietly left that country and returned home together. The father's daring plan to find and free his daughter had succeeded! His child was now safe in his arms at last.

In God's story of redemption, you are that child, Sara. You see, God created Adam and Eve to start the human race. Their rejection of God's rule over their lives plunged all mankind into the worst slavery of all—total bondage to sin and to Satan. Now we, their descendants, are born with that same rebellious sinful nature. Like Adam and Eve, we have run away from God, seeking a better life on our own, apart from Him, only to find that our rebellion has led us into the very clutches of Satan, who holds us as prisoners under his control.

Seeing our desperate need for redemption, God devised a bold plan. He sent His Son into this hostile, foreign world, bound to sin and Satan and notorious for its slavery. Jesus became one of its citizens, and in His passionate pursuit of us, rescued us by offering the highest bid at enormous cost—His life![3]

Through redemption, He rescued us from being held captives by Satan. Christ outbid Satan for the possession of our souls—buying us back and recovering His rightful ownership.

Clearly we should have no doubt about how much He loves us, how valuable we are to Him, and how He longs to have us in His family.

Unlike the father in the story who only risked his life, Christ gave His life for our ransom—His life for ours.[4] Death on the cross was the ransom price of redemption that He paid to release us from bondage in order that the divine justice of a holy God might be satisfied.

FREEING US FROM SIN'S POWER

Christ's death also paid the price to unshackle us from the addictive and enslaving power of sin.[5] Simply put, sin is character—specifically, the reflection of Satan's character in our lives. We sin when we allow behavior opposite to that of the character of God to be expressed through our words and actions.

The sinful nature that we are born with, that we inherit from Adam, contains this evil character. At its core is pride and self-will that rebel against God, dethrone Him from ruling over our hearts, and cause us to live independently of Him. In reality, we seek to make ourselves god. This is exactly what the high-ranking angelic defector Satan did.[6] And we blindly follow his example!

Our choice to allow sin to express itself through us begins like a seedling that sprouts in our hearts. As we feed and nurture it, it takes deeper root, becoming habitual, until it tries to invade other areas of our lives as well. Eventually the addictive nature of sin begins to hold us in its grip, making it very difficult to free ourselves in our own power. It is like being caught in an undertow or riptide in the ocean. Jesus, Himself said, *"Everyone who sins is a slave to sin."* [7]

Spiritual blindness sets in, and so does guilt and shame. Left unconfessed, our sins will eventually lead to death and eternal separation from God.[8] We are in desperate need for someone to set us free. Christ broke sin's power on the cross and made it possible for the Holy Spirit to live inside of us when we give our lives to Him Now we can be set free from sin's control to do God's will, with the power of the Holy Spirit at work within us.

PAYING THE PENALTY OF THE OLD TESTAMENT LAW

Through His death, Christ also redeemed us from the curse and penalty of the Old Testament Law.[9] God gave this Law to Moses, and it is contained mainly in the books of Exodus and Leviticus. The Law embodied the whole essence of God's legal requirements, and it warned that if a person violated the Law in just one point, they were guilty of breaking it in all points, thereby resulting in the curse of death.[10]

Obviously no one could flawlessly keep God's laws. Consequently we all stood hopelessly judged under the Law, and the death sentence rested upon us. Jesus, however, having fulfilled the Law perfectly through His sinless life,[11] became a curse for us and paid the penalty for our violation of the Law. His righteousness could now be put to our spiritual account so that we could be set free from its sentence of death.

It would be equivalent to this scenario: Imagine yourself in a federal courtroom. You have just been convicted for breaking the law and are given the death sentence. As you await your turn to be executed on death row, something unbelievable happens. One day the warden comes to your cell and unlocks it, saying, "You're free to go." "On what grounds?" you ask in bewilderment. He responds, "A man named Jesus has taken your place and has satisfied the legal requirements for your violation of the law."

On the cross, Jesus broke the chains of every bondage and addiction for us. He liberated us from every hostile power. Our complete deliverance has already been paid for and acquired. What a debt of gratitude we owe our Redeemer! When we truly realize how much Christ loves us and the great price He paid to set us free, we too, like Sara to her father, should fall at His feet and freely offer our lives to Him in devoted, loving service.[12]

However, misinformation and misconceptions can rob us of this deliverance. When President Abraham Lincoln emancipated the slaves in 1863, some slaves thought it was too good to be true. Thinking that it was a deceitful plan to kill them once they left their masters, they continued to live in the horrors of slavery when they could have walked away as free people. Unfortunately, many Christians live this same way, failing to recognize that they have been freed.

Christ has provided for victory over sin's power in our lives. He has overcome Satan and his demonic forces—taking their spoils and offering freedom to their captives.[13] The jail door has been unlocked and opened. All that remains for us to be free is to believe Christ and, by

faith, walk through the prison door and into freedom. There He eagerly waits to receive us into His family.

If you have not yet experienced Christ's redemption, you can do so right now. Turn to page 161 for a prayer to guide you. Receive the gift of redemption that Christ offers you! The alternative is to remain enslaved to sin, Satan, and death.

REDEMPTION—
A TREASURE FROM THE CROSS

ENDNOTES

1. Genesis 4:7; John 8:34-36; Romans 6:6
2. 2 Timothy 2:25-26
3. Galatians 1:3-4; Ephesians 1:7-8; Titus 2:14; 1 Peter 1:18-20
4. Matthew 20:28; 1 Timothy 2:5-6; Hebrews 9:15
5. Revelation 1:5
6. Isaiah 14:12-15; Ezekiel 28:12-17
7. John 8:34 (NIV)
8. Isaiah 59:2; James 1:15
9. Galatians 3:13; 4:4-5; Ephesians 2:14-15; Romans 8:1-4; Colossians 2:14
10. James 2:10; Galatians 3:10; Deuteronomy 27:26
11. Hebrews 4:15; Matthew 5:17-18
12. 1 Corinthians 6:19-20; 2 Corinthians 5:15
13. Colossians 1:13-14; 2:15; Luke 11:20-22

HISTORICAL INSIGHT INTO THE CRUCIFIXION

Who was responsible for killing Jesus?

1. Judas Iscariot (Mark 14:43-46; John19:11)

2. The Jewish religious leaders—although they had not the power to do it themselves (John 18:31; Matthew 27:20-23, 25; Mark 15:9-11)

3. The Roman Procurator Pontius Pilate (who gave the order) and his soldiers (Matthew 27:24, 26; Luke 23:20-25)

4. God the Father (Isaiah 53:4, 10; Acts 2:23; John 3:16; 19:10-11)

5. You and I indirectly—it was because of our sins that He died (Isaiah 53:5-6; Matthew 26:28)

Note also that Jesus voluntarily laid down His life (Mark 10:45; Matthew 26:53-54; John 10:17-18; Galatians 1:4; 1 Timothy 2:6; Titus 2:14).

It just so happens that we were all involved in His death!

CHAPTER 10

RESCUED FROM ETERNAL DESTRUCTION:
SALVATION

*Those who passed by hurled insults at him, shaking their
heads and saying, "You who are going to destroy the temple
and build it in three days, save yourself! Come down from the
cross, if you are the Son of God!"*

*In the same way the chief priests, the teachers of the law and
the elders mocked him. "He saved others," they said, "but He
can't save Himself! He's the king of Israel! Let him come down
now from the cross, and we will believe in him."*

Matthew 27:39-42

I F Jesus had come down from the cross miraculously and saved Himself, He would not have been able to save us. Christ could not have saved us by living. He could only save us by dying—and then being raised to life again.

Has anyone ever asked you, in a religious sense, if you were saved? Did you wonder what in the world they were talking about? Saved from what? It sounds as if it has already taken place—whatever it is!

LOST AND IN DANGER

Often, during His earthly ministry Jesus painted a picture of mankind as being lost in a wicked, hostile world where the power of sin and Satan's hatred threaten to destroy us. Jesus even summed up His mission by saying, *"For the Son of man came to seek and to save what was lost."*[1] This word *"lost"* in the Bible means the hopeless loss, not of being, but of well-being—in a condition of everlasting suffering.

Christ compared fallen humanity to lost sheep,[2] straying from their shepherd and in danger of predators—dangers so certain that it was only a matter of time before their complete destruction came to pass. The Bible states that *"your enemy the devil prowls around like a roaring lion looking for someone to devour."*[3] We can be saved from these dangers only by returning to the protective care of Jesus, our Shepherd.

Again, if we were to see fallen mankind through the eyes of Christ, we would hear Him say, *"Wide is the gate and broad is the road that leads to destruction, and many enter through it. But small is the gate and narrow the road that leads to life, and only a few find it."*[4] Jesus said this to teach us that the majority of people are deceived about the direction of their lives and do not see the great danger ahead of them. He implied that there will be more people going to hell than going to heaven. Clearly, Jesus tried to warn us of the danger.

Judgment Day will be a day of ruin for the majority of people who, for the most part, are completely unaware of this reality.[5] Like a crew on a boat moving down an uncharted river, they have no idea that the river ends abruptly in a massive waterfall plunging hundreds of feet below. Or like sailors at sea on a ship at night with a broken compass and cloudy skies, they are drifting aimlessly in the darkness, oblivious that they are on a collision course with a deadly coral reef.

God Sent Someone to Save Us

God saw that we were helpless to save ourselves from certain destruction, and in His great mercy and love He sent Jesus to earth to seek and to save our perishing race.[6] Jesus' very name means Savior,[7] and it was through passionate love, much pain, and extreme self-sacrifice that He sought us and died for us. In God's sight we were of such worth and value that He chose to give His Son to save us.

However, we may not even realize that we need to be saved. We may be blinded to the truth that destruction looms ahead. We may even think such talk of destruction and becoming *"saved"* is foolishness.[8]

But picture a man driving one day along a busy highway. The weather is bitterly cold. Suddenly he sees a little dog in the middle of the road. He just has to stop! Through heavy traffic, he hurries to rescue the dog, which is shivering and crying bitterly. After very nearly being hit by several cars, the man makes his way to the dog, but the dog runs away. Again and again he almost catches that half-frozen animal, but each time it escapes his grasp. Finally there is nothing more he can do. He has to give up!

This situation is a lot like ours. The more God tries to save us from the impending danger we face, the more we may run away from Him. Instead of running into His protective care, we flee. God could say, "I died for you. I have pursued you. I have done everything an omnipotent God could do to try to save you, but you would not let me! You just would not let me!"

ESCAPING THE DESTRUCTION

The only way to avoid this disaster is to decide to let Him save us. We do this through repentance and turning our lives over to Jesus Christ. We must get off the "broad road" to destruction and onto the "narrow road" to safety. It only takes **a sincere decision** to change our direction. When that decision is made, God will save us.

Consider again that ship about to hit a coral reef. If the captain sees a lighthouse in the distance, he has the choice to continue drifting aimlessly in the unknown waters and risk ruin, or turn toward the lighthouse, averting the calamity that lies ahead in the direction of the coral reef.

Or consider again the boat drifting down the river toward the waterfall. If the crew members want to be saved from the waterfall, they must turn around before passing the point of no return. Likewise, we must turn to God before it is too late, or else meet with certain destruction.

By faith, we must change our course to safety while there is still time.[9] Jesus will help us to do this. The choice now rests with us. What rejoicing there is in heaven when one sinner repents and is saved![10]

So if you and I repent of our sins and trust in what Jesus accomplished on the cross for us, we will be saved...

...from the enslaving power of sin into a life free from bondage.

...from Satan's power into the safety of God's protection.

...from future judgment in the lake of fire into the security of God's heavenly kingdom.[11]

Are you saved?

If you confess with your mouth, "Jesus is Lord," and believe in your heart that God raised him from the dead, you will be saved. For it is with your heart that you believe and are justified, and it is with your mouth that you confess and are saved. As the Scripture says, "Anyone who trusts in him will never be put to shame."...for, "Everyone who calls on the name of the Lord will be saved." [12]

If you have not yet had a salvation experience, you can have one right now. Turn to page 161 for a prayer to guide you.

SALVATION— A TREASURE FROM THE CROSS

ENDNOTES

1. Luke 19:10
2. Luke 15:3-6; Isaiah 53:6
3. 1 Peter 5:8 (NIV); 2 Corinthians 4:3-4
4. Matthew 7:13-14 (NIV)
5. Revelation 20:11-15
6. John 3:16-17; 1 Timothy 2:3-4
7. Matthew 1:21; John 10:9; Acts 4:12; Romans 5:9-10
8. 1 Corinthians 1:18-25; 2:14
9. Ephesians 2:8-9; Titus 3:4-6
10. Luke 15:7, 10
11. Mark 9:43-48
12. Romans 10:9-13 (NIV)

MEDICAL INSIGHT INTO THE CRUCIFIXION

"Not uncommonly, insects would light upon or burrow into the open wounds or the eyes, ears, and nose of the dying and helpless victim, and birds of prey would tear at these sites. Moreover, it was customary to leave the corpse on the cross to be devoured by predatory animals. However, by Roman law, the family of the condemned could take the body for burial, after obtaining permission from the Roman judge."

Edwards et al., "On the Physical Death of Jesus Christ," 1460.

CHAPTER 11

ESCAPING DIVINE JUDGMENT:
MERCY

From the sixth hour until the ninth hour darkness came over all the land. About the ninth hour Jesus cried out in a loud voice, "Eloi, Eloi, lama sabachthani?"—which means, "My God, my God, why have you forsaken me?"

Matthew 27:45-46

DURING His life, Christ bore the shame and disgrace of illegitimacy. Then He left the world bearing the shame of a criminal, humiliated in the presence of His mother and loved ones as He hung there naked before them.

Christ was well acquainted with rejection and abandonment. His half brothers did not believe in Him.[1] His hometown of Nazareth did not accept Him.[2] After all that His disciples experienced with Jesus, they still abandoned Him at the most crucial hour of His life.[3]

Furthermore, His own Jewish nation, from whose lineage He prophetically descended and for whom He came to save and present Himself as Savior and Messiah, rejected Him and crucified Him. Now as He hung on the cross with the sins of the world weighing Him down, and

as He writhed in unimaginable torment, the unthinkable happened: His own Father in heaven turned His back on His Son and forsook Him.

"Why have you forsaken me?"

Had Christ's Father really deserted Him at this most critical moment of His life? Or was it just a feeling of abandonment caused by the fever, weakness, and pain that Jesus endured on the cross?

The key to the answer is found in Christ's question, "Why?" Isaiah tells us that, *"He was pierced for our transgressions, He was crushed for our iniquities; the punishment that brought us peace was upon Him... and the Lord has laid on Him the iniquity of us all....we considered Him stricken by God, smitten by Him, and afflicted...yet it was the Lord's will to crush Him and cause Him to suffer."* [4] Yes, Jesus really was forsaken by God on the cross. He was forsaken because He was bearing our sins.

The Scripture tells us that God cannot look upon sin, but rather His anger and judgment must be poured out upon it. Since Jesus stood in our place, His Father treated Him as a sinner, and God the Father withdrew His Presence from His Son, forsaking Him on the cross—breaking the perfect fellowship they had enjoyed throughout eternity.

THE FATHER'S ANGUISH

We also know from Scripture that God's heart can be touched with our pain. [5] Watching His only Son hang on a cross in agony certainly wrenched His heart. In a small way, God allowed the patriarch Abraham to experience a degree of this anguish when He tested Abraham to offer his only son, Isaac, as a sacrifice, who was a type of Christ. [6]

No one will ever fully comprehend God the Father's heartache when the intimacy between Him and His Son was broken on the cross.

Imagine His added grief at having to also pour out His anger upon His Son as Christ became an object of sin for us all!

But the Father could not intervene. If He did, He would have aborted the plan of salvation *"from the creation of the world"*[7]—the only remedy for our sins. The Father gave up that which is the most precious to Him to have mercy on us. How can we ever doubt His love for us?

WHAT JUDGMENT DO WE ESCAPE?

What is the nature of this judgment from which Christ saved us? When Jesus walked this earth, it seemed as if He talked more about hell than He did about heaven. He described it as a place so frightful that the demons, who will one day be there and already have a glimpse of it, are terror-stricken at the thought of going there.[8] Hell is so dreadful that the rich man (who was in hell) earnestly begged Abraham to warn his brothers back on earth so that they wouldn't end up where he was.[9]

Hell is so terrifying that Jesus said it would be better for a person not to have been born than to end up there.[10] Christ also said that hell is so horrifying that it would be better to give up a part of our body if it would cause us to go there.[11] The Bible describes it as a place where there is no light but only darkness;[12] no freedom but only confinement;[13] no love or joy but only weeping, wailing, and mourning[14]—a place where there is no comfort but everlasting torment.[15]

Hell is indescribable. We cannot fathom a place where people are jailed forever without parole or any chance of getting out; where no prayers are ever answered and no mercy is ever shown; where there is bitter remorse and regret; where there is no place to hide or escape to;

where there is no hope but dark despair; and where unbelievers will exist forever with Satan and his demonic spirits.

Some may rationalize that eternal punishment is overkill, that it doesn't "fit" the offense. The fact that God would allow His only Son to pay such an awful price to save us proves conclusively that there *must* be a dreadful future for those who die in their sins.

TRANSFER OF SIN

How was the judgment that should have come upon us shifted onto Christ? This transfer of judgment was foreshadowed for us in the Old Testament feast of Passover. As we see in Exodus 12, the first Passover took place while the Israelites were slaves in Egypt. Each household was to kill a lamb without defect and apply its blood on the front door of their homes. God said, *"When I see the blood, I will pass over you."* In so doing, the Israelites escaped God's wrath and judgment.[16]

In the New Testament Jesus became our Passover Lamb.[17] Christ voluntarily received the full force of His Father's wrath for our sins while He was on the cross so that we might escape His judgment and experience His mercy. Because God has **already** poured out His wrath toward us upon the person of Jesus, His judgment doesn't have to come upon us.

If we are under the protection of Christ's blood, God's judgment will *pass over* us, but if we refuse to transfer our sins onto Jesus, we will continue to bear them, giving God no other alternative but to bring His judgment upon us. Jesus said, *"Whoever believes in the Son has eternal life, but whoever rejects the Son will not see life, for God's wrath remains on him."*[18]

Jesus was forsaken that we might be accepted by God and might never know what being absolutely forsaken and deserted by God is like. There has never been a lonelier person than Jesus separated from His Father on the cross so that we would never have to be separated from God again.

Jesus bore the wrath of God that we might escape being ultimately sentenced to the lake of fire. Jesus has already taken care of our sin on the cross, and if we receive this remedy, by faith, we will escape the judgment of God. There is no other way, for the Bible says, *"How shall we escape if we ignore such a great salvation?"*[19]

GOD'S SAFETY ZONE

There was an old railroad worker who had lived on the American prairie and told of his experience with a wildfire. He described the way in which he watched the Indians save their wigwams from the blaze through a technique that today is called a "firebreak." It is still used nationwide by firefighters. In this method, the Indians would *fight fire* **with** *fire* by deliberately setting flame to the dry vegetation immediately adjoining their settlement.

He went on to describe how the oncoming, raging inferno roared out of control as it came bearing down upon them—bringing death ever so close! But they would all take their stand in the burnt area, where their fire had already been. They had no fear, because there really was no danger—there was nothing left for the fire to burn. As a result, all were safe!

The reason God pleads with us and calls us to the cross is because it is the only place where the fire of God's judgment has already burned.

His Son took this judgment once for all, and it will never come upon Him again. The person who takes his stand beneath the cross of Christ is safe forevermore and at perfect peace within the protection of God's safety zone.[20]

Are you safe and protected from God's judgment and out of harm's way? If not, you can be. Turn to page 161 for a prayer you can pray to receive God's mercy.

MERCY—
A TREASURE FROM THE CROSS

ENDNOTES

1. John 7:5
2. Luke 4:16-30; Matthew 13:53-58
3. Matthew 26:56
4. Isaiah 53:4-6, 10 (NIV)
5. Judges 10:16; Isaiah 63:9; Genesis 6:5-6
6. Genesis 22:1-19
7. Revelation 13:8; 1 Peter 1:19-20
8. Luke 8:26-33; Matthew 8:28-29
9. Luke 16:27-28
10. Matthew 26:24
11. Mark 9:43-48
12. Jude 1:13; Matthew 8:12
13. Luke 16:26
14. Matthew 13:40-42
15. Luke 16:22-24
16. Exodus 12:13, 23
17. 1 Corinthians 5:7
18. John 3:16-21, 36 (NIV); Mark 16:15-16
19. Hebrews 2:3 (NIV); John 8:24
20. Romans 5:9-10; 8:1-2; 1 Thessalonians 1:10; 5:9-10

MEDICAL INSIGHT INTO THE CRUCIFIXION

Beyond the excruciating pain, the major effect crucifixion had on the body "was a marked interference with normal respiration, particularly exhalation. The weight of the body, pulling down on the outstretched arms and shoulders, would tend to fix the intercostal muscles in an inhalation state and thereby hinder...exhalation."

"Adequate exhalation required lifting the body by pushing up on the feet and by flexing the elbows and adducting the shoulders. However, this maneuver would place the entire weight of the body on the [bones and nerves of the feet] and produce [unimaginable] searing pain. Furthermore, flexion of the elbows would cause rotation of the wrists about the iron nails and cause fiery pain along the damaged median nerves....Muscle cramps...of the outstretched and uplifted arms would add to the discomfort."[1]

However, "with the weight of the body being exerted on the feet, pain in the feet and legs mounted. When the pain became unbearable, the victim again slumped down on the sedulum with the weight of the body pulling on the wrists and again stretching the intercostal muscles. Thus the victim alternated between lifting his body off the sedulum in order to breathe, and slumping down on the sedulum to relieve pain in the feet. This tiring, agonizing respiratory cycle would continue throughout the ordeal."[2]

"Lifting of the body [up and down in this manner] would painfully scrape the scourged back against the rough wooden stipes," causing more blood loss. "Christ spoke seven times from the cross. Since speech occurs during exhalation, these short, terse utterances must have been particularly difficult and painful."[3]

---

1. Edwards et al., "On the Physical Death of Jesus Christ," 1461-1462.
2. N. P. DePasquale, G. E. Burch, "Death by crucifixion," *Am Heart J* 66 (1963): 434-435.
3. Edwards.

CHAPTER 12

GOD'S ANTIDOTE FOR SIN:
CHRIST'S BLOOD

I am poured out like water, and all my bones are out of joint.
My heart has turned to wax; it has melted away within me.
My strength is dried up like a potsherd, and my tongue sticks
to the roof of my mouth; you lay me in the dust of death....
a band of evil men has encircled me, they have pierced my
hands and my feet. I can count all my bones; people stare and
gloat over me. They divide my garments among them and
cast lots for my clothing.

Psalm 22:14-18

Note: These words were prophetically given to the psalmist David nine
hundred years before Christ's birth in Bethlehem.

Then the Lord sent venomous snakes among them; they
bit the people and many Israelites died. The people came to
Moses and said, "We sinned when we spoke against the Lord
and against you. Pray that the Lord will take the snakes away
from us." So Moses prayed for the people. The Lord said to
Moses, "Make a snake and put it up on a pole; anyone who is
bitten can look at it and live."

Numbers 21:6-8

Jesus said: "Just as Moses lifted up the snake in the desert, so the Son of Man must be lifted up, that everyone who believes in him may have eternal life."

John 3:14-15

A Christian radio program featured a retired minister who shared a fascinating story about a medical missionary he once knew. The missionary's name was Dr. Andrew, and he served on the African mission field, greatly helping the tribal village that God had called him to.

One day Dr. Andrew took his son Bobby and his son's friend Juma on a hiking trip into a wilderness area in Central Africa. They packed ample supplies for the weeklong trip and were excitedly anticipating the adventure. The trip was uneventful, except for the time their boat tipped over in the shallow, swift stream on their first day out. Even though they lost a few of their supplies, they made it to their destination safely and without further incident.

Later in the week, the two boys were gathering sticks to make a fire for that evening's meal. As they reached for kindling among some debris, suddenly both boys were struck and bitten by a snake.

The father heard the boys' frantic cries for help, and grabbing his gun and knapsack of medical supplies, he ran over to where they were. As he came upon the boys, he quickly assessed the grim situation. First he shot and killed the snake. It was a black mamba—one of the deadliest and fastest multiple-striking snakes known to man.

He carried the boys to a safer location away from the debris. They were a great distance from the nearest medical facility, and Dr. Andrew knew they would never get there in time, so he began to administer initial first-aid procedures to them there. Time was of the essence!

He hurriedly searched through his knapsack to find the antidote for a black mamba snakebite. To his horror, he discovered that he had enough antivenin to treat just ONE person. He realized he must have lost the rest when the boat had capsized.

His heart pounded. A feeling of anguish gripped him. He was faced with the most crucial decision of his life, and the pressure of this decision weighed heavily upon him. To which boy would he administer the antivenin? The seconds were ticking. He had to decide quickly.

The neurotoxic venom was beginning to show its effects upon the boys' cardiovascular and nervous systems as paralysis set in. He had to act fast! He explained the dilemma to his son, and together they came to a decision.

Dr. Andrew filled a syringe with the only dose of antivenin and shot it into the arm of his son's friend, Juma. As he did this, it was as if a knife went through his own heart. Grief-stricken, he rushed to his son's side, cradled Bobby's head in his lap, and began consoling him and telling him how much he loved him.

The father watched helplessly as his son drooled and frothed at the mouth and blood trickled from his nose. Bobby's chest and throat muscles were tightening as he gasped to breathe and struggled to stay alive. Then, in this nightmarish ordeal, the dreaded moment came. His son gave his final death throe and died in his father's arms from suffocation.

Dr. Andrew embraced his son and wept bitterly over the loss of his boy. A part of him had now died too.

His mourning was interrupted by a voice crying out behind him. He turned and saw that Juma was on his way to recovery. The antivenin was working!

Snake antivenin is made by injecting an animal with the poisonous venom of a specific kind of snake. The animal's immune system responds by generating cells to battle the invading toxin, which in turn produces antibodies to neutralize the poison. This antibody-rich blood is drawn from the living animal and the antivenin is extracted. It is now able to be given to anyone who has been bitten by that species of snake, causing the venom to lose its power to infect that person. This is what saved Juma.

The next day, when Juma fully realized what the father had done, he asked in utter bewilderment, "Why would you choose to save me instead of your own flesh and blood?"

The father answered, "Well, Juma, I was willing to let my son die because we both knew that Bobby was right with God and that he would immediately go to heaven. But we could not bring ourselves to let you die when we knew that you were unprepared for death—facing an eternity of judgment in hell without Christ. So I sacrificed my son with the hope that you would choose to put your faith in his Savior and live your life for God."

The host of the radio program was deeply moved by this account. When the man's story had concluded, he asked his guest, "I have one question. Do you know what ever became of Juma?" The elderly minister paused a moment. Then, with a quiver in his voice, he replied, "I am Juma, Bobby's friend, and I did not disappoint God."

This story illustrates what happened on the cross two thousand years ago. God, the Father, sacrificed His Son Jesus so that we could be spared from eternal damnation, which results from the venom of sin. Not only that, He sent His Son to defeat the *source* of that venom—Satan himself, the serpent. And just like Dr. Andrew, it caused the Father great pain and agony to sacrifice His Son—and yet, He did it. Try as we may, we could never imagine His pain.

Ponder for a moment how much God loves you. He would rather exchange the life of His Son for your life! Even more, consider God doing this with only the "hope" that you would hear this message and respond by choosing to serve Him (with the free will He has given to you). Like Juma, only you hold the answer as to whether the "risk" God has taken will pay off in your life, although He foreknows what you will do. Will you disappoint Him? Or will you, like Juma, receive the gift of His Son, give your life to Him, and serve Him forever?

Jesus Christ took our venomous sins upon Himself on the cross. He then shed His blood, which became God's antivenin for the sins of all mankind. Christ is the only One in the universe who has the antidote to neutralize the poison of sin in our lives so that it does not kill us for eternity.

But like any antidote, Christ's antidote is only effective if we **receive** it. Have you received it? This antidote—the shed blood of Christ—is God's only life-saving remedy for our sins. If you have not yet received it and would like to do so now by faith, please turn to page 161, where you will find a prayer to help you.

CHRIST'S BLOOD—
A TREASURE FROM THE CROSS

MEDICAL INSIGHT INTO THE CRUCIFIXION

Crucifixion wrought havoc on the cardiovascular system. Much blood loss and no liquid intake caused dehydration, resulting in a decrease in the amount of fluid in the vascular system. The blood would begin to thicken and, coupled with low blood volume, this would put the heart under tremendous strain as it tried to pump the syrupy-like blood.

Thickened blood, however, does not circulate well through the body, and with less and less blood left to pump, the heart of a person being crucified could not deliver an adequate supply of oxygen to the cells that were crying out for it.

Abnormal carbon dioxide levels in the blood due to the inability to fully exhale would combine with other waste products building up in the muscles, which the kidneys and sweat glands were having a difficult time removing. These toxins, together with fatigue, would create the onset of painful muscle cramps (much like a charley horse), which would hinder respiration even further.

As a result, the respiratory muscles in the chest would eventually become paralyzed, making breathing almost impossible. The condemned one eventually came to the point where he could no longer lift his body, and he usually died of suffocation (asphyxia).

Medical Aspects of the Crucifixion (video), hosted by Dr. Jameso Fuzzell
(Good News Productions, International, 1984).

CHAPTER 13

DIRECT ACCESS TO GOD:
MEDIATION

Jesus called out with a loud voice, "Father, into your hands, I commit my spirit." When He had said this, he breathed his last.

Luke 23:46

At that moment, the curtain of the temple was torn in two from top to bottom.

Matthew 27:51

I N Jerusalem stood the spectacular, breathtaking Jewish temple. It rivaled the seven wonders of the ancient world. What an awesome sight it must have been to gaze upon this colossal structure with its glistening gold and white marbled walls.

Located in the center of the temple was a room called the Most Holy Place, also known as the Holy of Holies.[1] Since the temple's inception around 963 BC, the Most Holy Place housed the renowned ark of the Covenant—a small rectangular wooden structure overlaid with gold, with two cherubim facing one another at each end, their outspread wings hovering over the sacred chest.[2]

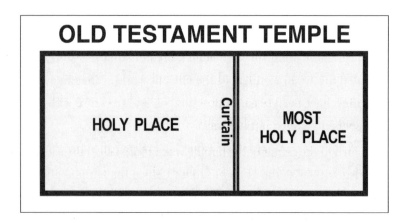

It was here, over the ark in the Holy of Holies, that the visible presence of God dwelt. The ark was a visual reminder to the Israelites that God was residing with them. In times past, His presence was manifested in this area as a cloud by day and a fire by night. But in the rebuilt temple of Christ's day, we are told that the only thing left in the Holy of Holies was a large stone, signifying where the ark had once stood. (The ark disappeared when the Babylonians destroyed the temple around 586 BC, and it still has not been found to this day.) The stone was used in place of the missing ark for the sprinkling of the blood of sacrificial animals.[3]

A huge four-colored curtain separated the Most Holy Place from the adjoining Holy Place. The Holy Place was where the priests performed their daily duties to the Lord. In it stood the seven golden lampstands, the table of showbread, and the altar of incense. The only time that anyone was permitted to enter beyond the curtain into the Most Holy Place was on the annual Day of Atonement (also known as Yom Kippur).[4]

On that solemn, momentous day, the High Priest was required to enter that sacred room to present sacrificial blood to atone for his own sins, his family's, and those of the entire Jewish nation.[5] Anything done there in the presence of God, contrary to His written instructions, meant instant death to the priest.

THE SIGNIFICANCE OF THE CURTAIN

In Christ's day, the curtain in the temple towered sixty feet high and spanned thirty feet wide, and it was very thick and heavy.[6] It was part of God's original blueprint for the building of the temple that He supernaturally communicated to Moses and King David.[7] The curtain was designed by God to illustrate the great wall of separation that exists, because of sin, between fallen man and an infinitely holy God This barrier prevented us from directly entering into God's presence and necessitated that someone represent us as a mediator before God. It also served as a reminder that heaven was inaccessible to us, as sinners, unless a way could be found for us to enter.

As Jesus died on the cross, that curtain in the temple was miraculously torn in two. The very presence of God was now suddenly accessible to everyone![8] Christ removed the barrier of sin through His work on the cross, and the curtain was no longer necessary.

The most amazing thing about the tearing of this curtain is that it suddenly tore on its own from top to bottom. This destruction of the curtain was clearly the work of God's hand. It would have been impossible for anyone to tear this thick sixty-foot curtain from top to bottom.

Jesus died at 3 p.m.—the time when the evening sacrifice began. God made sure that the priests were there so that they could be eyewitnesses to this incredibly amazing event. This event essentially meant that they were now out of jobs. The purpose of the office of priesthood had now come to an end, and there was no more work for them to do. A new order now replaced the old—a better and higher Priest had taken their place. Their office and duties had simply typified, or foreshadowed, the work that Christ performs for us in heaven as our Great High Priest and mediator.[9]

The Jews continued the Levitical priesthood with its sacrifices after Christ's death, but God personally brought this Old Testament system to a close some forty years later in AD 70. The Roman army under Titus besieged Jerusalem and burned and leveled the temple. It has never been rebuilt, but there are plans to resurrect it once more as Christ's

Second Coming draws near and as the church age and *"the times of the Gentiles"* come to a close.[10]

The elimination of the priesthood meant that God could now be approached directly through Jesus, the only mediator between God and men.[11] No more denied access to the presence of God under the threat and fear of instant death, we can now come to our loving heavenly Father through Jesus. No longer do we need a human intermediary to approach God on our behalf. In fact, we **cannot** come before Him through any other mediator than Christ. Jesus said He is the only door to God.[12] He also said, *"I am the way and the truth and the life. No one comes to the Father except through me."*[13]

THE BARRIER OF EXCLUSION

There was also another barrier separating Jew and Gentile. Keep in mind that the only way a person could be made right with God in the Old Testament was through keeping the Law of Moses and its Levitical sacrificial system. Therefore, a Gentile, or a non-Jew (one not descended from Abraham), had to adhere to this system in order to be brought into right relationship with God.

Once a person entered through the gates of the temple, that person was only allowed to go so far. The entire temple compound was considered holy, but it became increasingly more holy as one proceeded further in, from east to west, closer to the Most Holy Place.

As barriers of exclusion, the various courts represented the degree of a person's acceptable relationship with God. These several courts were constructed in such a way to restrict a person's access. Each court was elevated above the others, with the Most Holy Place occupying the highest point on the temple mount.

First there was the Court of the Gentiles, where any non-Jew who had proper respect for the temple could enter. Since the Gentiles were considered the farthest away from God, they were given the court that was lowest and farthest from the Holy of Holies.

The next court was for the Jews alone. At its entrance was a sign forbidding Gentiles to enter under the penalty of death. Archaeologists have discovered fragments of this warning etched in stone.

Then there was the Court of the Women. Any properly purified Jewish man, women, or child could enter here. Beyond that was the Court of Israel, which was for Jewish men only. Women were excluded from going any further because men were considered more righteous than women, simply because of their gender.

Next was the Court of the Priesthood, reserved for members of the priesthood. The innermost court, the Holy of Holies, was God's court.[14]

Warning Inscription

"No foreigner is to go beyond the balustrade and the plaza of the temple zone; whoever is caught doing so will have himself to blame for his death which will follow."

Source:
Tchinly-Kiosk Museum, Constantinople

No human being could enter here except the High Priest, and he could only do so one day a year on the Day of Atonement.

Christ's work on the cross changed all of this! He eliminated this system of exclusion and made us all equal before God! Now we can approach Him individually, on our own through God's prescribed way. Now both Jew and Gentile, male and female—all of us regardless of social class—can come into God's presence. On the cross, Christ *"destroyed the barrier, the dividing wall of hostility, by abolishing in his flesh the law with its commandments and regulations....For through him we both have access to the Father by one Spirit."* [15]

Christ tore down *"the dividing wall of hostility"* between Jew and Gentile, as well as the death sentence for any Gentile who tried to enter the inner courts of the temple. He also abolished the ordinances of the Old Testament ceremonial legal system. The Mosaic Law was intended to keep the Israelites morally pure in a decadent world, so that they could be witnesses of the true God and the vehicle through which Christ would come into the world.

But the Law also became the cause of bitter animosity between Jew and Gentile as it gave the Jews a sense of superiority that they flaunted and that the Gentiles detested. Since the Law as a means of salvation is no longer valid, however, the reasons for the enmity between Jew and Gentile have ceased to exist.

That is unbelievably fantastic news for us Gentiles today, who were once considered outcasts and aliens! When the Jews rejected the salvation Christ offered them, God turned to the Gentiles to offer it to them and to call out of them a people for His name, to become part of His church. He will continue to do this throughout the present church age until He turns His attention to dealing with the nation of Israel again in the future.[16]

No longer would the temple in Jerusalem be the only place people could worship God.[17] This temple was only a type of the temple in heaven, into which Christ has entered as our High Priest.[18] The church has replaced the Jewish temple. Christ's sacrificial death on the cross ushered in a new age in God's relationship with mankind.

In the New Testament, the Christian's body is now the temple of the Holy Spirit where the Presence of God resides.[19] Collectively, the church is the temple of God, comprised of all *"born again"* believers from all nations worldwide. Believers in Christ are now the *"living stones"* who make up God's temple.[20] And speaking of priceless treasures, the Presence of God is one of the most awesome richest blessings we mortals could ever have the privilege of experiencing. For in God's Presence we enjoy the peace and satisfaction that our spirit has longed for, divine guidance, and sacred fellowship with our heavenly Father.

WE CAN NOW APPROACH GOD

By coming to the Father through the merits of Christ's work on the cross (and not on our own merits), we are now encouraged in the New Testament to approach God confidently, boldly...and often.[21]

Think about what it would take to have a personal face-to-face meeting with the President of the United States. The probability of doing so would be very, very slim. But if by chance it could be arranged, imagine how long you would have to wait. You would have to undergo security clearances, be placed on hold for prolonged periods on the phone, and tolerate a lot of red tape. While we may need to endure all of this to see an important person in public office, through Jesus we can now have immediate access to God, the King of the universe, any time—day or night—simply through prayer! And He will hear us!

Furthermore, not only will He hear us, but Jesus assures us of answered prayer. He says, *"My Father will give you whatever you ask in my Name....Ask and you will receive, and your joy will be complete."*[22] The most powerful Being in the universe will now work to meet our needs! Think of it!

Christ has also made us a *"royal priesthood,"* to offer up prayers for others.[23]

Not only this, but now, as our great High Priest in heaven, Jesus Himself intercedes to His Father for us—and we know that He intimately understands our human experience and needs.[24] We can find strength in the fact that just as Christ prayed for Peter before he had committed the sin of denying Him so that his faith would not fail as a result of that trial, He will also pray for us. Imagine the power of Christ's prayers on our behalf!

He also pleads and defends our cause as an advocate before His Father. When we sin and our fellowship with God is broken, *"we have one who speaks to the Father in our defense."*[25] Admitting our guilt, Christ makes the case that He has already paid for this debt of sin on the cross and therefore forgiveness should be granted. When we confess our sin to Him, He restores our fellowship with God.[26]

Christ also defends us against Satan, our accuser. When Satan presents allegations against us, Christ represents the believer before His Father.[27] And when we experience long trials and mistreatment from others, Christ ensures that justice is served for His children who cry out to Him day and night.[28]

Christ is truly a wonderful advocate and mediator—a Great High Priest who has removed the barriers between God and us and who continues to mediate for us day and night.

MEDIATION—
A TREASURE FROM THE CROSS

ENDNOTES

1. Hebrews 9:1-5; 2 Chronicles 3:8-14

2. Exodus 25:10-22; 37:1-9

3. James Orr et al., *International Standard Bible Encyclopaedia* (1939; rpt. Grand Rapids: Wm. B. Eerdmans, 1974), Vol. V, 2938.

4. Exodus 26:31-33; Hebrews 9:6-7

5. Leviticus 16:1-34

6. Alfred Edersheim, *The Life and Times of Jesus the Messiah* (Grand Rapids: Wm. B. Eerdmans, 1965), Vol. 2, 611.

7. Exodus 25:1-9; 26:30; 1 Chronicles 28:1-21; Acts 7:44; Hebrews 8:5

8. Ephesians 2:11-3:6; Galatians 3:28-29; 1 Corinthians 12:13

9. Hebrews 7:23-8:2

10. Luke 21:24

11. 1 Timothy 2:5

12. John 10:9

13. John 14:6 (NIV)

14. "Herod's Temple," www.bible-history.com/jewishtemple/ (accessed July 2007).

15. Ephesians 2:14-18 (NIV); Acts 21:27-32

16. Acts 15:13-18

17. John 4:21-24
18. Hebrews 8:5; 9:24
19. 1 Corinthians 3:16-17; 6:19-20; 2 Corinthians 6:16-18
20. 1 Peter 2:4-10
21. Hebrews 10:19-23; 1 John 5:14-15
22. John 16:23-24; 15:7 (NIV)
23. 1 Peter 2:9
24. Hebrews 4:14-5:10; 7:25; Romans 8:34, 26-27
25. 1 John 2:1 (NIV)
26. 1 John 1:9
27. Luke 22:31-32
28. Luke 18:7-8

MEDICAL INSIGHT INTO THE CRUCIFIXION

Crucifixion was designed to be a lingering death. The length of survival on the cross ranged anywhere up to "four days and appears to have been inversely related to the severity of the scourging."

"However…the Roman soldiers could hasten death [within minutes] by breaking the legs below the knees," a method called crucifracture (see John 19:31-33). As those being crucified were unable to push up with their legs to get air, this would place the burden of exhalation on shoulder and arm muscles alone and soon would result in exhaustion asphyxia.

Edwards et al., "On the Physical Death of Jesus Christ," 1459, 1462.

CHAPTER 14

ETERNAL LIFE WITH GOD:
HEAVEN

And when Jesus had cried out...in a loud voice, he gave up his spirit. At that moment the curtain of the temple was torn in two....The earth shook and the rocks split. The tombs broke open and the bodies of many holy people who had died were raised to life.

Matthew 27:50-52

Jesus said..., "I am the resurrection and the life. He who believes in me will live, even though he dies."

John 11:25

MOST people do not realize that they become eternal beings the moment they are conceived in their mother's womb.[1] At that point, it is too late to turn back the clock. Eternal existence has begun!

Again, some would think we cease to exist as persons when our bodies die. According to the Bible, however, this is not true. Your physical body is the house in which your soul and spirit reside.[2] When your body dies, you continue to exist. But the question is, where will your soul and spirit go when they leave your body?

The Bible says that we are born with a spiritual condition that is dead toward God due to sin.[3] We are dead in our relationship to God. If we die in this condition, we will *"perish"* forever—suffering a conscious existence of torment in the lake of fire, forever separated from God's life and presence.[4]

Yet thank God, there is hope! The moment we receive Christ, He makes our spirits alive. Jesus puts into us His life and His nature. We actually become a *"new creation," "born again"* into an alive spiritual existence.[5] Then, when we die, we will continue to live eternally with God.

How does this happen? Scripture teaches that *"the life of a creature is in the blood."*[6] We have learned that one of the principles upon which biblical sacrifice rests is this: Sin is transferred to a substitute, and, in turn, the life (and innocence) of the substitute is transferred to the sinner. It was upon this principle that Jesus shed His sinless blood on the cross as our substitute, and thereby transferred His eternal life (and righteousness) to every believer.[7]

WHAT HAPPENS WHEN WE BECOME "BORN-AGAIN"?

When the life of God's Spirit enters our lives, He awakens our spirits toward God. We begin to respond to Him with a hunger and a thirst for God's presence, for **only** in Him is fullness of joy and perfect contentment found. That "God-shaped vacuum" within each of us that Blaise Pascal wrote of is now filled by Him. We develop an appetite for the Bible, God's written Word, which is the food that will nourish our spirits.[8] Truth is revealed by the Holy Spirit, and our spiritual blindness gradually starts to lift. The desire to pray and to communicate with God begins to grow.

The longing to please God is demonstrated by a desire to obey God and to do His will. We begin to hate evil and to love what is righteous and good. The fruit of the Spirit starts to grow and is produced in our lives.[9] The power of the Holy Spirit is manifested through our witness, our spiritual gifts, our serving others, and our giving of ourselves and our possessions. All these things are the direct result of Christ's life now working in us. Our spirits have been made **alive** to God! We have been regenerated.

At death—if Jesus does not return first—we will go directly to live with the Lord until the final resurrection. Then we will be given new bodies prepared for eternal life with Him. In the unimaginably glorious new heavens and new earth that God has promised, God *"will wipe every tear from their eyes. There will be no more death or mourning or crying or pain"*—only joy and peace in His wonderful presence.[10]

ILLUSTRATING ETERNITY

How long is eternity? Imagine a great bird that could fly nonstop without ever needing to rest. Let us say that it were possible for this bird to fly to the planet Jupiter at one mile per hour. Let's pretend that God gave this huge bird an assignment: "Take every grain of sand from planet Earth to Jupiter—**one at a time!**"

Picture this huge bird as it takes the first grain of sand in its beak and begins to flap its enormous wings. Envision it lifting off the ground and flying upward and upward until it disappears into the sky. It arrives 44,520 years later at Jupiter—a distance of 390 million miles from

earth—and upon landing, drops the first grain of sand onto the planet. Then immediately, it makes the return trip to Earth—a round-trip of 780 million miles, or 89,040 years, for just one grain of sand.

How many years would it take to transport every single grain of sand off the face of the earth in this manner? Whatever it is, it would not even scratch the surface of eternity. When the bird returns from taking the last grain of sand to Jupiter, eternity would still be as long as it was when he had left with the first grain of sand!

PREPARING FOR ETERNITY

Because every person will spend this eternity either with God in heaven or without Him in hell, it is eternally and critically important that we prepare to go to heaven. Like planning for any trip, we need to make decisions and preparations. However, many of us give little thought or planning to where we will travel once our bodies die. Where will your soul and spirit go when your body is dead?

The Bible teaches that we will either go directly to heaven or directly to hell when we leave our bodies.

Have you given any thought to where you are going? If not, let's think about it for a moment. The road map is simple. The Bible says that we are on one of two roads—the wide road leading to hell or the narrow road leading to heaven.[11] Choose which route you will take.

What can you take with you? Nothing tangible of course, but there *are* things you will be taking into the next life. According to Christ's true account of the rich man who went to hell, we will retain our memory and recognition of others, as well as our ability to see, hear, reason, speak, and sense things.[12] We will also take our relationships with us, and a record of the things we have done and said—later to be judged.[13]

Have you made a reservation for heaven, yet? If not, you can do so by calling on Christ and becoming a child of God. The only payment that will allow us admittance into heaven is Christ's payment. He is also the only door through which we can enter.[14]

When standing on the brink of death, a believer has the assurance of Christ's promise that angels will be there to carry him over death's waters to heaven's shore, so that he can live with Christ forever in that glorious land.[15] In anticipation, true Christians will live their lives with faith in that promise, in God's character, and in the Bible.

Once we are born, we will exist forever. The question is, "Where?" If you want to have the certainty that you will live forever in heaven, turn to page 161 for a prayer to guide you in securing your eternity with God.

"God has given us eternal life, and this life is in His Son. He who has the Son has life; he who does not have the Son of God does not have life." [16]

HEAVEN—
A TREASURE FROM THE CROSS

ENDNOTES

1. Jeremiah 1:4-5; Psalm 139:13-16; Luke 1:13-15, 36, 39-44
2. 1 Thessalonians 5:23; Hebrews 4:12; Matthew 10:28
3. Ephesians 2:1-5; Colossians 2:13
4. Revelation 20:11-15; John 5:24, 28-29; John 3:16
5. 2 Corinthians 5:17; John 3:3-5
6. Leviticus 17:11
7. John 17:1-3, 24; Romans 6:23
8. John 6:63; Deuteronomy 8:1-3
9. Galatians 5:22-24
10. Revelation 21:1-4 (NIV); John 10:27-29
11. Matthew 7:13-14
12. Luke 16:19-31
13. 2 Corinthians 5:10; Matthew 12:36-37; 16:26-27; Revelation 14:13; 20:11-13
14. John 14:6; 10:1-9
15. Luke 16:22
16. 1 John 5:11-13 (NIV)

MEDICAL INSIGHT INTO THE CRUCIFIXION

What was the cause of Christ's death? Although the actual cause involved many contributing factors such as exhaustion, the effects of scourging, blood loss, dehydration, and hypovolemic shock,[1] there are several medical theories as to the final cause:

Theory #1: Asphyxiation. Some believe Jesus died primarily of asphyxiation due to exhaustion and muscle paralysis, the usual cause of death in crucifixion.[2] However, some counter this theory by saying that because Jesus spoke and cried out in a loud voice just before He died (Matthew 27:50; Mark 15:37), it is questionable whether He could have done that while suffocating, seeing that there was not a complete "shut down" of his lungs.

Theory #2: A ruptured heart. There is a membrane or sac that surrounds the heart muscle called the pericardium. As the body undergoes great stress and the heart continues to struggle to pump the remaining sluggish blood, the amount of fluid increases in this sac through edema. As the pericardium slowly expands with fluid, it compresses the heart, placing on it more pressure and causing an excruciatingly deep crushing pain in the chest cavity.

The Bible states that the soldiers pierced Christ's side with a spear to ensure that He was already dead (John 19:34). We are told that *"blood and water"* immediately flowed out. This is probable indication that the pericardium had been punctured since no other organ in the area of the spear thrust would have contained sufficient "water," except the pleural cavity around the lungs. If both blood and water were indeed in the pericardial sac, this would be a strong indication that His heart ruptured and that some of the blood from the heart went into the pericardium.[3]

Theory #3: Cardiorespiratory failure. Due to all the contributing factors listed above, cardiorespiratory failure could have occurred due to a sudden loss of blood to the heart caused by something like a blood clot in a major vessel. The failure also could have been due to a deprivation of oxygen in the bloodstream, so that the heart was no longer capable of functioning.[4] "A fatal cardiac arrhythmia [a disruption in the regular beating of the heart] may have accounted for the apparent catastrophic terminal event."[5]

Some believe this theory makes it harder to satisfactorily answer what caused both *"blood and water"* to flow from Christ's side after His decease. Although the source of the *"water"* could still have come from the pericardium [or the pleural cavity], some say that depending on how long it was from the point of death to the insertion of the spear, there would not have been much fluid in the blood for it to run out because of its thickened state and its tendency to clot faster. [6]

1. Edwards et al., "On the Physical Death of Jesus Christ," 1461, 1463.
2. N. P. DePasquale, G. E. Burch, "Death by Crucifixion," 434-435.
3. Information obtained through interview with Dr. Jameso Fuzzell, July 2007.
4. Information obtained through interview with Dr. Jameso Fuzzell, July 2007.
5. Edwards et al., "On the Physical Death of Jesus Christ," 1463.
6. Information obtained through interview with Dr. Jameso Fuzzell, July 2007.

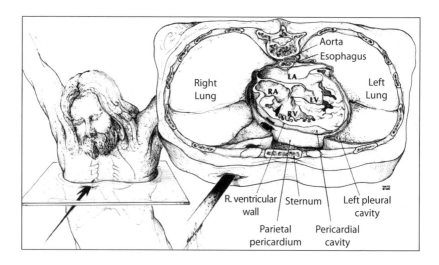

Spear wound to chest. *Left,* Probable path of spear. *Right,* Cross section of thorax, at level of plane indicated at left, showing structures perforated by spear. LA indicates left atrium; LV, left ventricle; RA, right atrium; RV, right ventricle.

CHAPTER 15

LIVING VICTORIOUSLY FOR CHRIST:
SPIRITUAL EMPOWERMENT

There was a violent earthquake, for an angel of the Lord came down from heaven and, going to the tomb, rolled back the stone and sat on it....The angel said to the women, "Do not be afraid, for I know that you are looking for Jesus, who was crucified. He is not here: He has risen, just as he said."

Matthew 28:2, 5-6

But God raised him from the dead, freeing him from the agony of death, because it was impossible for death to keep its hold on him.

Acts 2:24

I am the Living One: I was dead, and behold I am alive forever and ever! And I hold the keys of death and Hades.

Revelation 1:18

All authority in heaven and on earth has been given to me.

Matthew 28:18

But when this priest had offered for all time one sacrifice for sins, he sat down at the right hand of God. Since that time he waits for his enemies to be made his footstool.

Hebrews 10:12-14

P ART of Christ's great work on the cross was to make power available to us for overcoming the enemies that try to destroy us: sin, Satan, and death. God has a timetable for eliminating each one of them.

THE VICTOR OVER SIN

Christ is the victor over sin. Sin is a deadly enemy because its power enslaves us, harms other people, and separates us from God. But having broken the power of sin, Jesus can enable us to live a victorious life over sin. We no longer have to live a lifestyle that makes sinning a hopelessly habitual practice.[1]

Take Nicky Cruz for example. Born to witchcraft-practicing parents in Puerto Rico, he suffered severe physical and mental abuse at their hands during his childhood. Bloodshed and mayhem were common occurrences in his life. Full of anger and rage, he traveled to New York City at age fifteen and eventually became the president of the notorious Brooklyn street gang known as the Mau Maus. He fearlessly ruled the streets as warlord of one of the gangs most dreaded by rivals and police. Nicky was arrested countless times and lost in a cycle of drugs, alcohol, and brutal violence until God got his attention through the life of a street evangelist, David Wilkerson, and Nicky was marvelously saved and delivered. Nicky dedicated his life to Christ, and his ministry now reaches troubled youth worldwide—and has been doing so for fifty years.[2]

Or take an ordinary person like Jack, my dad, who, for various reasons, became addicted to alcohol, which caused domestic violence and other family dysfunctions. He gave the empty fragments of his life to Christ in 1967, and God has empowered him to live a victorious Christian life and be able to celebrate over forty years of sobriety!

Then there is Annie Lobert. Feelings of low self-esteem, rejection, and brokenheartedness plagued her constantly throughout her difficult childhood due to abuse. She never felt loved. Betrayal by her high school boyfriend and their subsequent breakup was the last straw. Deeply hurt and devastated, Annie rebelled and entered the promiscuous pop culture lifestyle and began her search for love and acceptance.

Annie tried sex to feel wanted and loved, but it resulted in more hurt, bitterness, anger, and rejection, which inadvertently led to prostitution and an eleven-year-long nightmare as a high-class call girl in Las Vegas. Gradually she became a slave to the sex industry, experiencing sex addictions, the pain of miscarriages and abortions, severe physical and emotional abuse by her clients and pimp, jail time, and much worse. She had a bout with cancer, leading to addiction to prescription pain medication, which led to taking drugs of every kind to deal with her bitter disappointments. Annie hated what she had become. Nothing she tried satisfied that empty need inside her.

Annie came to a point where she had so much pain, anger, shame, guilt, regret, and disillusionment in her life that she just wanted to end it all! One night she overdosed. As death and fear crept in, her life flashed before her. In that dark moment, Annie instinctively cried out for help to the Jesus she had learned about in her childhood. She promised that if He saved her life, she would tell the whole world about Him. Christ had mercy on Annie.

Shortly thereafter, she dedicated her entire life to Christ when she discovered that He loved her unconditionally. The power of God is now healing and transforming her and satisfying that need within. God has since called her into a ministry outreach to help prostitutes and anyone in the sex industry to see that their lives can be transformed by Christ just as hers was. [3]

There are countless others who have similar stories of the power of God at work in their lives—all because of Christ's victory over sin.

Sin's grip enables satanic powers to hold men captive. This is the secret of the devil's strength over mankind. But when Jesus broke the power of sin through His death on the cross, He disarmed the powers of darkness so that they could no longer use sin's power to master us.

THE VICTOR OVER SATAN

Immediately after Adam and Eve sinned in the garden, God addressed Satan through the serpent: "*And I will put enmity between you and the woman, and between your offspring and hers; he will crush your head, and you will strike his heel.*"[4] God promised to send a Deliverer who would conquer Satan and his demonic spirits.

This Scripture was fulfilled on the cross. God, in His wisdom, chose to defeat Satan openly through Christ's death and resurrection.[5] Satan played a role in Christ's crucifixion, depicted by the nail piercing His feet and heel, but through His death and resurrection, Jesus crushed the head of the serpent, Satan, and defeated him and all his forces. Only Christ could have conquered him.

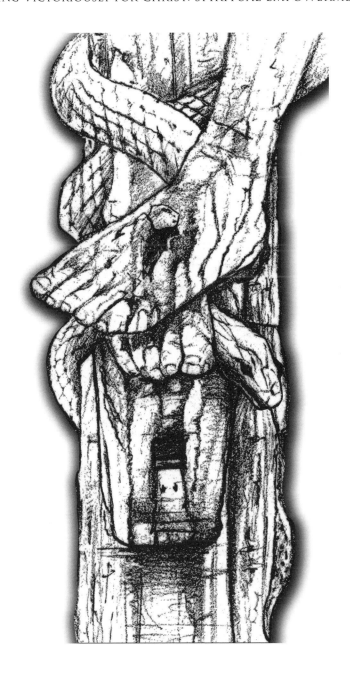

The cross, which seemed like a symbol of weakness, was turned into a symbol of triumph over all the powers of darkness. As a result, all demonic spirits will be cast one day into the lake of fire.[6]

However, for the time being, Satan *"prowls around like a roaring lion looking for someone to devour."*[7] Indeed, he still rules this world system. He targets us for destruction and makes this world a place of constant danger.

But Jesus came to earth for the express purpose of destroying the evil works of the devil.[8] Those things in our lives that Satan intends for evil, God specializes in turning into good. Having defeated Satan on the cross, Jesus now gives us His authority and the power of His Holy Spirit to resist and to overcome the power of the devil—not only in our lives but also in the lives of others.[9]

We also have no need to fear the devil or demonic spirits. Jesus gives His children divine protection over the powers of darkness. As we stay under His blood—God's hedge of protection—satanic spirits can do nothing to us outside of the permission and knowledge of God. And no one but ourselves can snatch us out of the eternal grip of the Father's hand.[10]

THE VICTOR OVER DEATH

Because of Christ's sinless life, death could not hold Him in the grave.[11] Death held no claims on Him. Jesus said, *"I am the resurrection and the life. He who believes in me will live, even though he dies."*[12] Indeed, it is the resurrection of Jesus that gives the proof to all His claims. His death would not have meant anything had it not been for His resurrection.

"Then Simon Peter...went into the tomb. He saw the strips of linen lying there" (John 20:6).

Through His death, Jesus broke the power of death.[13] During His earthly ministry, Christ raised a number of people from the dead through the Holy Spirit's power—Jairus' daughter, the widow's son, and His friend Lazarus to name a few.[14] The power of the Holy Spirit also moved through Christ's disciples, who also raised people from the dead.[15] God's resurrection power is still being manifested today, as it was when Jesus walked this planet.

In November 2001, Nigerian pastor Daniel Ekechukwu was fatally injured in a car accident near the town of Onitsha, Nigeria. As he was taken to the nearest hospital, he lost all life signs and was later pronounced dead by two different medical staff in two different hospitals. A medical report was written up, and the corpse was sent to the mortuary.

God reminded Nneka, his wife, of a verse of Scripture from Hebrews 11:35: "*Women received their dead raised to life again.*" By extraordinary faith, she insisted that the coffin containing his body be brought to a meeting in a local church where the Reverend Reinhard Bonnke was scheduled to preach. The rest is history. God raised Daniel to life again in one of the most astounding miracles of our time.[16]

He also freed us from being enslaved to the fear of death.[17] Now we can face death with the assurance that God will be there to receive us with open arms. Having broken death's power, Jesus makes it possible for us to have everlasting life with Him. If we become one with Him by dying to sin, we shall also rise from the dead as He did and live with Him forever.[18]

Furthermore, having this glorious hope, we are commanded by Jesus to store up our treasures in heaven, where nothing can ever take them away. As we overcome our spiritual enemies, He promises to reward us in heaven for our obedience—every thought, word, and deed.

We can experience Christ's power in our day-to-day trials as well. Just as surely as day follows night and spring follows winter, with trust in God and perseverance, we can count on Him to bring blessings out of our darkest and seemingly most hopeless circumstances—bringing forth life out of death—no matter how bleak things appear to be. If only we could see the other side like Jesus did, who by faith looked beyond His sufferings to the joy of victory that would follow.[19]

What enemies our conquering Christ has defeated! How crushing was the defeat He handed them! His body will forever bear the marks of the crucifixion, as a reminder of His victory and of the price He paid for our salvation.

There is no greater power than the power of Jesus. We can overcome anything with His help. By receiving Jesus and by accepting His sacrificial work on the cross, we can have the power of God's Holy Spirit—the same power that created the universe and raised Jesus from the dead—working in our lives to overcome the enemies of sin, Satan, and death.

SPIRITUAL EMPOWERMENT— A TREASURE FROM THE CROSS

Note: If you want to learn more about how to practically wage spiritual warfare using the weaponry Christ has provided to us, and if you have a desire to be empowered with spiritual breakthrough in your life, please check out my DVD series and workbook entitled *The Armor of God: Winning the Invisible War,* available on my website at www.DiscoverMinistries.com.

ENDNOTES

1. Romans 6:6
2. Nicky Cruz, *Run, Baby, Run* (Gainesville, FL: Bridge-Logos Publishers, 1988). See www.nickycruz.org for more information.
3. Retrieved on April 4, 2009 from www.myspace.com/annielobert
4. Genesis 3:15 (NIV)
5. Colossians 2:15; 1 Peter 3:22
6. John 12:31; 16:11; Matthew 25:41; Revelation 20:10
7. 1 Peter 5:8 (NIV)
8. 1 John 3:8
9. Luke 9:1; 10:19-20

10. John 10:28-29
11. Acts 2:24-27
12. John 11:25-26 (NIV)
13. Hebrews 2:14
14. Mark 5:22-23, 35-43; Luke 7:11-15, 22; John 11:43-44; 12:1
15. Matthew 10:1, 5-8; 11:4-5; Acts 9:36-42; 20:9-11; John 14:12
16. "Raised from the Dead" (video), (Orlando, FL: Christ for All Nations, 2002). See www.cfan.org for more information.
17. Hebrews 2:15
18. Romans 6:5; 8:11; 1 Corinthians 15:21-26, 54-55
19. Hebrews 12:2

MEDICAL INSIGHT INTO THE CRUCIFIXION

The power and reality of God can be seen in His ability to convey future events through human beings. Below are just some of the astounding prophesies about Jesus the Messiah, written up to 1,500 years before His birth. For a frame of reference: BC stands for "before Christ"; AD stands for "*anno domini,*" Latin for "the year of the Lord." The Old Testament (BC) years count down to the year of Christ's birth; the New Testament (AD) years count up. Christ died about AD 33.

Scriptures Foretelling Christ's Arrival, Death, & Resurrection

Old Testament Prophecy	Approximate Year Given	Event Fulfilled
Immanuel, "God with us," will be born of a virgin – Isaiah 7:13-14	730 BC	Matthew 1:20-23
He will be born in Bethlehem – Micah 5:2	720 BC	Luke 2:1-7
The week in which the Messiah would present Himself as king and die, and the destruction of Jerusalem in AD 70 – Daniel 9:24-26	500 BC	Luke 19:28-44; 21:5-6, 20-24
He will ride on a donkey as King – Zechariah 9:9	500 BC	Matthew 21:1-7
Betrayal by a close acquaintance... – Psalm 41:9	1000 BC	Luke 22:47-48
...For 30 pieces of silver – Zechariah 11:12-13	475 BC	Matthew 26:14-16; 27:3-10
His disciples flee and desert Him – Zechariah 13:7	475 BC	Matthew 26:56
He will be silent before His accusers – Isaiah 53:7	700 BC	Matthew 27:12-14

Old Testament Prophecy	Approximate Year Given	Event Fulfilled
He will be beaten, mocked, scorned, and ridiculed – Isaiah 50:5-6 Psalm 22:6-8	700 BC 1000 BC	Matthew 26:67; 27:26-31, 39-44; Luke 22:63; 23:11
His hands and feet will be pierced – Psalm 22:16	1000 BC	Luke 23:33; 24:39-40; John 20:19-20, 26-27
He will be treated as a criminal – Isaiah 53:12	700 BC	Mark 15:27-28
They will divide His clothing and cast lots – Psalm 22:18	1000 BC	Mark 15:24
There will be darkness at noon – Amos 8:9	780 BC	Matthew 27:45
He will experience exhaustion and thirst and will be given wine vinegar to drink – Psalm 22:14-15; 69:21	1000 BC	John 19:28-29
He will be forsaken by His Father in heaven – Psalm 22:1	1000 BC	Matthew 27:46
He will commit His spirit to His Father – Psalm 31:5	1000 BC	Luke 23:46
He will die for others – Isaiah 53:5-8	700 BC	Matthew 20:28
Not a bone of His will be broken – Exodus 12:43-46; Numbers 9:9-12	1500 BC	John 19:32-36
He will be buried with the wicked in a rich man's tomb – Isaiah 53:9	700 BC	Matthew 27:57-60
He will arise from the dead – Psalm 16:8-11	1000 BC	Acts 2:29-33
He will ascend into heaven – Psalm 68:18	1000 BC	Acts 1:9-12; Ephesians 4:7-10

CHAPTER 16

NEVER ENDING COMMITMENT:
COVENANT LOVE

When he had led them out to the vicinity of Bethany, he lifted up his hands and blessed them. While he was blessing them, he left them and was taken up into heaven...before their very eyes, and a cloud hid him from their sight.

Luke 24:50-53; Acts 1:9

Jesus said: "In My Father's house are many dwelling places; if it were not so, I would have told you; for I go to prepare a place for you. If I go and prepare a place for you, I will come again and receive you to Myself, that where I am, there you may be also."

John 14:2-3 (NASB)

Then I heard what sounded like a great multitude...shouting: "Hallelujah!...For the wedding of the Lamb has come, and his bride has made herself ready."

Revelation 19:6-7

THE following story is taken from *Philosophical Fragments* by Søren Kierkegaard:

> Suppose there was a king who loved a humble maiden. The king was like no other king. Every statesman trembled before his power. No one dared breathe a word against him, for he had the strength to crush all opponents. And yet this mighty king was melted by love for a humble maiden.
>
> How could he declare his love for her? In an odd sort of way, his very kingliness tied his hands. If he brought her to the palace and crowned her head with jewels and clothed her body in royal robes, she would surely not resist—no one dared resist him. But would she love him?
>
> She would say she loved him, of course, but would she truly? Or would she live with him in fear, nursing a private grief for the life she had left behind? Would she be happy at his side? How could he know?
>
> If he rode to her forest cottage in his royal carriage, with an armed escort waving bright banners, that too would overwhelm her. He did not want a cringing subject. He wanted a lover, an equal. He wanted her to forget that he was a king and she a humble maiden, and to let shared love cross over the gulf between them.[1]

In a similar way, God desired true spiritual intimacy with our first parents, Adam and Eve, as well as with us, their descendants. They were created by God in His image and likeness without sin, and He placed them in a garden in Eden located at the headwaters of the Tigris and Euphrates rivers in the Middle East.[2]

God brought them into existence to have intimate spiritual fellowship with Him and to be recipients of His love. In return, He wanted their genuine love, obedience, and worship for who He was. They were also to produce offspring, like you and me, who would also live in fellowship with their Creator.

God knew that programming them like robots to love Him was not the way to achieve His goal of true love and service. Using His awesome power to force them to love and serve Him against their wills was not an option either. God desired to be loved and wanted for who He is—not for anything else.

In order to experience the kind of love He desired, God created them like His angels, with the freedom to choose. He gave them "free will," the ability and the authority to make their own choices whether to serve Him or not. By giving them this ability, God ran the risk of rejection, but it was the only way to obtain the genuine, voluntary love that He desired.

FAILING THE TEST

Though He foreknew what Adam and Eve would do, God tested their love and obedience to prove how real their commitment was to Him. He gave them one commandment, forbidding them to eat the fruit from a particular tree out of the many in the garden.[3]

Ignoring the terrible consequences of their actions, Adam and Eve chose to reject God's sovereign rule over their lives. They chose, instead, to believe the lie of Satan. He was the fallen angel Lucifer, who had led the angelic rebellion against God in heaven. Satan now spoke to them through the serpent in the Garden of Eden. Heeding his words, they disobeyed God's command and ate the forbidden fruit—sinning against God and "missing the mark" of the purpose for which they were created.[4]

You may be asking, "Why should I be concerned about all this? How does this affect me?" It affects you in every way! By rebelling against God, Adam and Eve robbed each one of us of God's original intent for mankind. Dethroning God from their lives resulted in the sin, evil, injustice, sickness, suffering, and death that has gripped our world ever since. The way they exercised their freedom of choice brought evil into our planet. And when they fell, God then drove them from the garden to work the ground, which He cursed. They and all their children would now die, and their bodies would return to the dust from which they had been created.

Thankfully, the tragic story doesn't end here. Before God banished them from the garden, He promised them a Deliverer, who would some-day defeat Satan and provide a way to escape death and destruction.[5] This Deliverer would be a sinless descendant of Adam and Eve—Jesus Christ.

GOD LOVES YOU THE WAY YOU ARE

Now think for a moment about the kind of love the king had for the girl in the story. His love was not the type that said, "I'll love you *if…*," or, "I'll love you *when….*" She was being courted by royalty simply for herself. Though others may have thought her unattractive, the king loved her just as she was. She did not need to **do** anything to make him love her.

Since he prized her as a valuable treasure, he devised a way to approach her. The king chose to descend to her level and to become a common citizen—renouncing his throne in order to win her hand. And with a worn cloak fluttering loosely about him, he approached her cottage incognito.[6]

Jesus, like this powerful king in our story, loved us so much that he chose to come down from His royal throne in heaven and lay aside the splendor of His kingly robes and equality with God.[7] Stooping down, He clothed Himself in ordinary, common garb as one of us, to win our hearts and love and to deliver us from our sins so that we could live with Him forever. But unlike the king in the story, He did this when we were despicable, unlovable enemies of His—our garments and hearts soiled with the filthy wretchedness of our sins.[8]

Have you ever wanted someone to love you just the way you are? Perhaps you have been fortunate in this life to have been the recipient of a genuine love like this from another human being. Or have you instead had the misfortune of painful, broken relationships? In either case, there is no one in the universe who values you more and loves you like Jesus Christ does. He loves you unconditionally, just as you are!

A KING IS PURSUING YOU

You may be oblivious to this incredible truth. Do you realize that the story of the powerful king and the lowly maiden is actually being played out in your life—even at this very moment? Yes, you are literally being sought after by a King! He is like no other king. He is the King of all kings, for all authority in heaven and on earth has been given to Him.[9]

You don't have to do anything to earn or deserve His love, nor do you have to go searching for Him. Christ, by His Holy Spirit, is already trying to woo you, knocking on your heart's door, seeking your love and obedience. He is calling you out from the masses, pursuing you to become part of His bride—His invisible, eternal church: the Body of Christ.[10] Contemplate this honor! How could you turn down this royal proposal from the King of the universe?

But you may be thinking that you do not measure up and qualify to be part of His bride because of your sins. Yes, Christ is looking for a bride that is pure and undefiled. The wonderful news is that He will enable you to meet His standards and qualify you in His sight in spite of your unloveliness—through His work on the cross. There is nothing standing in your way.

All you need to do to enter into this covenant relationship is to turn *from* your sins and turn *to* Christ's offer of betrothal and say "yes"— placing your faith in Christ for the forgiveness of your sins and receiving Him into your heart. God will take care of the rest.

When we say, "yes" to Jesus, He gives us His Holy Spirit as a pledge— or an "engagement ring," as it were—confirming that He is serious about His intentions toward us and assuring us of all He has promised.[11]

You can rest assured that when you become a child of God, you become a recipient of God's magnanimous love and commitment throughout eternity—a love that will be faithful and never fail. Think of it!

If you are not yet God's child, will you accept His marriage proposal? I realize that it is a big step to put your trust in someone you cannot see, but that is the way God has designed it. This is why only a small percentage of people find this treasure. But you can be one who does.

Do you need evidence that He is truly real? Trust the gentle tugging at your heart as the Spirit of God woos you right now. The presence of God that you sense is proof that He is alive. The Holy Spirit is asking for you to believe in the God of the Bible and in the work Jesus did for you on the cross.

He values and desires your love and obedience. Will you give them to Him? What do you have to give up? Nothing but those things that God will replace with priceless gifts a thousand times better! Say "yes" to Christ right now, and whenever you envision Him hanging on that cross, be reminded of His deep love for you and the terrible price He paid to try to win you and find a place in your heart.

Indeed, the fundamental message of the entire Bible is the story of God's relentless, passionate pursuit to restore the fellowship with mankind that was lost in the Garden of Eden, and the extent He would go to recover that relationship—even to the sending of His own Son to die to obtain it!

If you want to enjoy this kind of love, commitment, and security—forever—you can begin to have it right now. Turn to page 161 for a prayer that will guide you in saying "yes" to Christ's marriage proposal.

COVENANT LOVE—
A TREASURE FROM THE CROSS

ENDNOTES

1. Søren Kierkegaard, *Philosophical Fragments,* translated by David Swenson (Princeton, NJ: Princeton University Press, 1962), as paraphrased by Philip Yancey in *Disappointment with God* (Grand Rapids, MI: Zondervan, 1988), 103-104.

2. Genesis 2:8-14

3. Genesis 2:15-17

4. Genesis 3:1-19

5. Genesis 3:14-15

6. Kierkegaard, *Philosophical Fragments.*

7. Philippians 2:5-11

8. Romans 5:6-11; Colossians 1:21

9. Matthew 28:18

10. Ephesians 5:22-33; 2 Corinthians 11:2; Acts 15:14-17; John 10:27; Revelation 19:7-9

11. Ephesians 1:13-14

HISTORICAL INSIGHT INTO THE JEWISH MARRIAGE CUSTOM

To fully and accurately understand the relationship between Christ and His bride, the church, and to gain insight into Christ's Second Coming, a proper understanding of the Jewish custom of matrimony in Christ's day is essential. This custom is not given to us step-by-step in the Bible, but Christ has chosen to pattern the way He will deal with His church after this amazing, divinely inspired institution.

The Jews in the first century did not date like we do today. Marriage to them was a practical legal matter and consisted of a number of steps. Here is a partial overview of the ancient Jewish marriage process as it relates prophetically to Christ and His church:

Ancient Jewish Marriage	Christ and His Bride
1. *Selection:* When a young Jewish man saw the girl he wanted (or the girl his father said he wanted), he would leave his father's house and travel to the home of his prospective bride to present his marriage offer.	**1. *Selection:*** Christ left heaven, His Father's house, and came to earth, the home of His prospective bride, to present His marriage offer and to invite all people through His Holy Spirit to become a part of His church **(Acts 15:12-18).**
2. *Betrothal:* **A. *Contract:*** This was a covenant containing the "bride-price," the promises made by the groom to the bride, and the rights of the bride. **B. *Bride Price:*** The most important element was how much the bridegroom was willing to pay the girl's father for permission to marry her. It reflected her value, as well as the groom's love, and it compensated her father. The price was generally quite high. **(See Genesis 29:18.)**	**2. *Betrothal:*** **A. *Contract:*** The marriage covenant provided by Jesus is the New Testament. It contains the "bride price," provision for the forgiveness of sins, and the promises made to Christ's bride. **B. *Bride Price:*** Jesus, our Bridegroom, died on the cross and shed His lifeblood to purchase us **(1 Corinthians 6:19-20; Acts 20:28).**

Ancient Jewish Marriage	Christ and His Bride
2. *Betrothal continued*:	**2.** *Betrothal continued*:
C. *Cup of Acceptance:* If the terms were acceptable, the groom would set a cup of wine before the girl. If she drank, it indicated her acceptance. Upon payment of the purchase price, the marriage covenant was sealed. This betrothal legally bound them together as husband and wife, except for sexual union. The betrothal could only be broken by a bill of divorce for immorality or unfaithfulness. The groom departed by giving her gifts and with these reassuring words: "I go to prepare a place for you."	**C.** *Cup of Acceptance:* At the Last Supper, Christ set the cup of decision before us all. We accept Christ's offer when we say, "I do," by receiving Him as Savior and committing our lives to Him, even though we have never seen Him. Each time we partake of the bread and wine at communion, we reaffirm our engagement to Christ. Jesus departed with these assuring words: *"I go to prepare a place for you."* He also gave us the gift of the Holy Spirit—His "ring" or guarantee that He will return for us and perform all that He has promised **(John 14:1-3; 1 Corinthians 11:25; Matthew 26:27-29; Ephesians 1:13-14; Genesis 24:1-66).**

Ancient Jewish Marriage	Christ and His Bride
3. Consecrated Waiting Period:	**3. Consecrated Waiting Period:**
The **groom** returned to his father's house to build her a bridal chamber, which would usually take about a year. During this time, the bride and bridegroom would prepare for married life and would not see each other. The groom's father would be the final judge of when the chamber was finished and when the young man could go to claim his bride.	With the Ascension, **Jesus** returned to His Father's house in heaven. He has been away from His bride, the church, for two thousand years preparing a special place for her. Jesus taught that only His Father knows when He will return to take His bride to live with Him **(Mark 13:32-37)**.
The **bride** kept herself pure and wore a veil whenever she stepped out of her house so that other young men could see that she was "bought with a price" and "set apart" for marriage to her bridegroom.	The **church** is to prepare herself and maintain spiritual purity during this time. She is commanded to separate herself from the godless world system since she is "*bought with a price*" **(1 Corinthians 6:20)** and "set apart" exclusively for Christ, her bridegroom. Like the Jewish bride, it is possible to commit spiritual adultery against Christ during this waiting period **(2 Corinthians 6:14-18; 11:2-3; James 4:4; Ephesians 5:25-27, 31-32; Hebrews 12:14)**.
The bride lived in anticipation of the return of her groom, who could come at any time, usually during the night. Therefore, she had to be prepared to travel at a moment's notice. Her sisters and bridesmaids also waited expectantly with her.	The church should be living in anticipation of the return of her bridegroom, who could come at any moment, "*like a thief in the night*" **(1 Thessalonians 5:1-2)**. Christ's parable of the ten virgins waiting for the bridegroom teaches us of the need to be alert and ready for His return so that we do not miss it and get left behind **(Matthew 25:1-13)**.

Ancient Jewish Marriage	Christ and His Bride
4. *The Bridegroom's Return:* When the groom's father said it was time, his son summoned his friends to join him on the exciting trip to claim his bride. This was usually done at night so as to completely surprise her.	**4.** *The Bridegroom's Return:* When the Father says to His Son it is time to claim His bride, *"The Lord himself will come down from heaven, with a loud command, with the voice of the archangel and with the trumpet call of God, and the dead in Christ will rise first. After that, we who are still alive and are left will be caught up together with them in the clouds to meet the Lord in the air. And so we will be with the Lord forever"* (**1 Thessalonians 4:16-18; Matthew 25:6; Revelation 4:1**). This is commonly referred to as the **rapture** of the church. The signs of the end times given prophetically in the Scriptures forewarn the church of the season of His arrival.
Upon approaching her house, they were obliged to give her a warning. Someone would shout and blow the shofar, or ram's horn, announcing the groom's arrival.	
When the bride heard that shout, she knew she only had time to light her lamp, grab her honeymoon clothing, and go. Her bridal party also had to be ready. And so the groom and his men would charge in, grab the girls, and make off with them! The romantic part was that all the Jewish brides were "stolen" and carried off into the night.	Like the Jewish bride's groom, the church's Bridegroom will also arrive *"like a thief in the night"* and carry her off. When Christ's bride is taken to His Father's house in heaven, she will enter into spiritual union with Christ, thereby consummating the relationship that Christ began with the church at His Last Supper. The marriage supper of the Lamb will conclude the wedding celebration in heaven near the end of the seven-year period called Daniel's "seventieth week" (**Daniel 9:24-27; Revelation 19:6-9**).
Then they all traveled to his father's house, where the bride and groom entered their new chamber to consummate their marriage. Seven days later the marriage supper would take place, which concluded the wedding celebration.	

Note: Even more amazing parallels exist between Jewish marriage customs and the marriage of Christ and His church as presented in the New Testament. The reader is encouraged to unearth these exciting parallels through additional study.

Adapted from Zola Levitt, *A Christian Love Story* (Dallas, TX: Zola Levitt Ministries, 1978).

CHAPTER 17

"IT IS FINISHED":
MAKING THESE
TREASURES YOURS

When he had received the drink, Jesus said, "It is finished."
With that, he bowed his head and gave up his spirit.

John 19:30

WHEN Jesus cried out, *"It is finished!"* what did He actually mean? Perhaps to our surprise, this was really a shout of victory! He had completed His mission in perfect obedience to His Father, fulfilling the plan of redemption. Christ's one driving passion was summed up when He said, *"My food* [or reason for existence] *is to do the will of Him who sent me and to finish His work."*[1]

The Greek word used in the New Testament for *"It is finished"* is *tetelestai.* It is a legal accounting term meaning "paid in full." As archaeologists have unearthed ancient contracts and bills of sale in the Middle East, they have discovered this word written on many of them whenever the last installment had been paid—finishing the contract.

"It is finished!" Christ had finished satisfying God's just demands with regard to sin. He had completely defeated the forces of darkness on the cross, having waged tremendous spiritual warfare. All the Old Testament prophecies and promises concerning His first coming had

151

been fulfilled. All the animal sacrifices prescribed in the Old Testament Law, which foretold of His work on the cross, were now consummated in Him! Future sacrifices would be meaningless.

In finishing His great work of salvation for us, Jesus paid our sin-debt **in full**—never to be paid again! His substitutionary blood sacrifice for us was now perfect and complete. He has done it once and for all.[2] *"It is finished!"* How can we begin to add to or improve upon the work that Jesus so perfectly completed?

None of us can do anything to perfect Christ's work on the cross. But when we approach God for reconciliation on our terms, in a way that seems right to us, aren't we actually saying to Him that "my way is as good as the work that Jesus accomplished on the cross?" We may not consciously mean that, but in reality that is what we are saying. No amount of good deeds we could do could ever offset and pay the debt of sin we owe to God; we could never earn our way to heaven. Don't be fooled into believing that you can.

We have learned that the only payment God will accept to satisfy His judgment upon sin is the shedding of blood of an innocent victim in place of the guilty.[3] Christ is the only sinless One who qualifies to deliver mankind from his seemingly hopeless situation.[4] Bloodless sacrifices are unacceptable to God, just as Cain's was.[5]

We can only obtain salvation by trusting in Christ's work for us and not in any of our own works. Religious activities such as church attendance and membership, baptism, communion, charitable giving, the sacraments, and ritualistic prayers cannot atone for our sins. Good deeds are important as acts of obedience to be rewarded, but they will never merit our salvation.

The notion that good deeds can pay for or merit forgiveness of sins is a dangerous misconception. The good things we do will never qualify for one chief reason: They not only lack the critical element of a blood sacrifice, but they also imply that Christ's work fell short—as if we have to do more. Are we so bold as to suggest that when God gave us His only Son that He did not give enough? Or that Jesus did not do enough?

You may be thinking to yourself, "But surely, there *has* to be *something* I must *do!*" And there is—with God's help.

How to Receive These Priceless Gifts

The first step is to realize that the salvation God offers is conditional. Just because Jesus died for the sins of every person who ever lived does not mean that everyone is automatically forgiven and has been given a right standing before God. God waits for us to respond. Think of it this way: Just because there is enough soap in the world to clean every person doesn't mean every person in the world is clean. Why? Because not everyone has taken the soap and applied it.

Let me explain further. The word *testament* as used in both the Old and New Testaments indicates a covenant or contract. In any contract, there are at least two parties who vow to perform specific conditions as part of that agreement, in order to make the contract work. God requires that we enter into a covenant, or a contract, with Him.

The Old Testament was a covenant initiated by God with Israel, and only when Israel did not keep her part did the contract fail. God was always faithful to do His part. However, at the Last Supper, Jesus introduced something new. Referring to the cup of wine they drank at that Passover meal, Christ said, *"This is my blood of the new testament, which is shed for many for the remission of sins.*[6] In other words, He replaced the Old Testament based on animal sacrifices with the New Testament based on the sacrifice of Himself.

Christ has fulfilled His part of the new covenant through His finished work on the cross, and now He promises to help us as we fulfill our part of the New Testament, for we could never make it in our own strength. But that still leaves the question, how do we respond and become partakers of that new covenant? What is it that God is waiting for us to DO? It involves three parts: changing direction, believing in Jesus, and consecrating our lives to Christ.

CHANGE DIRECTION

To enter into this covenant relationship with God, we need to change direction. Jesus called this **repentance**. It involves a change of heart and mind. It is a decision to turn from walking in sin to walking with God instead. It also involves confessing our sins to God and asking Him for forgiveness.

Producing good fruit after this will prove our change of heart. We can change direction only with God's help, and we cannot do it without Him. It's like traveling on a bus and suddenly realizing that you are headed in the wrong direction. At the first opportunity, you must get off and get onto the right bus. [7]

BELIEVE IN JESUS

When asked what deeds God required a person to do to satisfy Him, Jesus replied to *"believe"* in His Father who sent Him. [8] In fact, Christ went on to say, *"if you do not believe that I am the one I claim to be, you will indeed die in your sins."*[9]

The true meaning of this word *believe* in the original Greek does not mean just a mere acceptance of facts, but a continual, lifelong trust and reliance upon Christ for salvation. It is a commitment to do God's will.

In 1859 Charles Blondin walked a tightrope 1,100 feet across Niagara Falls. The next year the Frenchman returned with his agent Harry Colcord. This time he wanted to increase the theatrics. Imagine the scene as Blondin challenged the crowd below, "Who believes that I can carry any of you across the Falls?" "Yes, I believe you can!" someone shouted back. "Then, come up here!" Charles demanded. But the man had second thoughts and backed out.

Charles called out his question again. This time there was no response from the crowd. Finally he challenged his agent, "Harry, you tell everybody that I can carry a man on my shoulders across the Falls. If you really believe it, will you be that man?" And before the eyes of thousands of gasping spectators, including the visiting Prince of Wales, Harry rode on Blondin's shoulders over the mighty Falls and back again as the thundering cascades plunged over the huge rocky cliffs below. Both men said they "believed," but only his agent demonstrated genuine belief by trusting and committing himself to Blondin's tightrope ability. The other man had shown only a mental agreement.

This story perfectly illustrates the difference between mere belief in facts and the kind of true trust and commitment that God is looking for.[10]

Like the different facets of a diamond, the word *believe* in its biblical sense includes all of the following:

- Being fully persuaded that Jesus is the Son of God and that He has been raised from the dead. (See John 8:24; Romans 10:9-11.)

- Transferring our sins onto Jesus as our substitute and Sin-Bearer.

- Receiving Christ into our hearts. We do this by inviting Him to reside in us so that the Spirit of Jesus, the Holy Spirit, literally comes into our being.[11] Our spirits become *"born again."*[12] We then step down from the throne of self-will and allow Christ to rule and take full control of our lives. He demands first place in our lives, and as we submit to Him, this results in the fruit of obedience to do His will. When we receive Christ, we receive all the precious treasures He provided on the cross.[13]

- Making an open, public confession to others of our allegiance to Christ that He is our Savior and the Lord of our life! The biblical command for water baptism is part of this acknowledgment.[14]

By repenting and believing, we begin our Christian life in the power of the Holy Spirit and enter into a covenant relationship with Jesus. But this is only the beginning of the lifelong process of being conformed to the character of Christ.

CONSECRATE YOUR LIFE TO CHRIST

Separating ourselves from sin and setting ourselves apart for God's use is a lifelong process. The biblical word for this process is *sanctification*. As part of the new covenant, Jesus calls Christians to *"walk worthy*"[15] and take up their crosses and follow Him.[16] What does this "cross" consist of? A normal cross is made when a horizontal crossbeam intersects with a vertical crossbeam. What Christ means by "taking up our crosses" is when God's will intersects with our wills on a given issue and we submit to His will, no matter what it costs us. This involves **daily** denial of our own wishes when they run contrary to God's and putting to death the evil desires that arise out of our fallen sinful nature in order that God's life in us can grow. It requires hating those things that appeal to our fallen nature and that are a part of the world system that is in rebellion against God.

Nature itself teaches us the principle that life comes through death. A bird hunts its prey. A fish gulps down another fish. A leopard stalks an antelope. Plants and animals must die every day to provide us with food.

> Life and death are the law of field, stream, and jungle.... The principle that nothing lives unless something else dies extends beyond nature to our daily walk with God. Interests of the flesh [sinful nature] must succumb to the interests of the [Holy] Spirit, or else the interests of the Spirit will succumb to the interests of the flesh. In the jungles and fields and streams of our own heart, something must always die so that something else can live.[17]

Without this personal "crucifixion" and obedience in our lives, sin will once again take control of us. And if we live in habitual sin, we will have failed to meet the conditions of the New Testament and we will be separated from God and prevented from living in heaven with Christ.

But thank God for His wonderful promise that He who has begun a good work in us will complete it to the end.[18]

As God empowers us through His Holy Spirit, He gives us the desire and the ability to do His will. When we walk in the power of the Holy Spirit, He produces the fruit of the Spirit in our lives, such as love, joy, and peace. And finally we have God's promise that when Jesus returns, we will see Him face-to-face.[19]

Repenting, believing, and separation from sin sum up our part of the New Testament and are the things God said we must DO so that we can be forgiven and enjoy eternity in heaven.

In the Bible, Jesus told a story about a treasure that was hidden in a field.[20] One day a man unexpectedly discovered it. Glancing around to ensure that no one was watching him, he quickly buried it again in a different place. With great joy and excitement, he returned to his home and proceeded to sell everything he owned to get enough money to purchase that field in order to gain possession of that treasure.

In a moment, he moved from poverty to proverbial riches. Only by recognizing that the value of his present possessions paled in comparison to that treasure could he then take the bold step to make the personal sacrifice to give up everything he had in order to obtain it.

Believe it or not, right now you are reliving this man's experience. You too have stumbled upon life's greatest treasure—Jesus Christ and His awesome love for you. Like this man, your next step will be determined by the value you place on this treasure. Today, you can experience this treasure—a personal relationship with God Himself!

But in order to discover this priceless gift from God, you must be willing to make the most important decision that you will ever make in your lifetime. That decision is to repent of your sins and to invite Jesus into your heart and choose to serve Him. Like the man in the field, you will need to "sell out" by giving up all rights to your life in order to gain possession of Christ. It is a choice you will never be ashamed of nor regret. Your spirit will awaken to new life and a new awareness of God, and you will be completely transformed.

Remember, all these priceless treasures that have been presented are found in the person of Jesus Christ, for it is in Him, and Him alone, that all these treasures lie hidden.[21] They cannot be obtained in any other way than by receiving Christ.

Christ's treasures from the cross are love gifts from God—to be received or to be rejected.[22] To be of any benefit, a gift must be received. The moment we begin to work for it, it ceases to be a gift. You may firmly believe that God wants to give you this gift, but unless you reach out and take possession of it by faith, you don't have it.

If you have not yet received Christ, His Holy Spirit is drawing you right now. If you cannot remember a time when you made a decision to commit your life to Him, then you probably haven't. Right now is your opportunity.

Having fulfilled His part of the New Testament through the finished work of Christ on the cross, God calls you to respond. He is now asking you to make a **decision**—to repent and believe—and to receive Jesus into your heart and make Him ruler over your life.

This is the most important decision you will ever make in your life, for it will determine where you will spend eternity. You have so much to gain by saying "yes"—and so much to lose by saying "no." And to make no decision at all *is* a decision; it's the same as saying, "No!"

God will not force you. Instead, Jesus lovingly knocks at the door of your heart and says, *"If anyone hears my voice and opens the door, I will come in."*[23] Again, He invites you, *"Come to me, all you who are weary and burdened, and I will give you rest."*[24] How can you turn down His invitation to become His child, to become a part of His kingdom? Don't allow pride, shame, or anything to keep you from turning your life over to Christ and miss this awesome treasure.

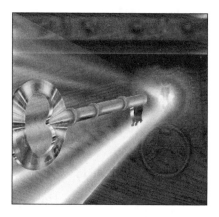

God does not want anyone to perish and go to hell. He desires that all would come to repentance and be saved from judgment.[25] You can receive Jesus Christ right now. It begins with a decision. The following prayer will help you make this decision. In effect, it's like turning the key that unlocks the treasure. These words have the power to transform your life. If you sincerely mean them, God will certainly respond to your prayer and reveal His reality to you.

He is waiting!

A PRAYER TO RECEIVE JESUS CHRIST

Dear Lord Jesus, I am a sinner. But I believe You died in my place on the cross and were raised to life again. Forgive me of all my sins. I turn my back on my past sinful life—vowing never to return. I renounce the devil and all of his works. I open the door of my heart to You. I invite You to come in and rule my life. I give up all rights to my life and I submit to your lordship. I receive You, by faith, as my Lord and Savior. I receive all the treasures You purchased for me on the cross.

With Your help I will keep my part of the New Testament. Show me Your plan for my life. Thank You for dying in my place on the cross and for forgiving all my sins. Thank You for making me Your child and for giving me eternal life with You forever. Amen.

If you have just received Jesus by praying this prayer, you have now entered into a covenant relationship with God. Your name has been written before God in His Book of Life.[26] The Bible says that you have become a new creation in Christ.[27] Though there may be ongoing consequences that continue from what you have sown in the past, your former life has been forgiven. You are now able to make a brand-new start! Just as a newborn baby has a new life ahead of him, so it is for you as well—you have been *"born again"* spiritually. Not only this, but all the wonderful spiritual treasures Jesus purchased by His death on the cross have become yours.

In order to maintain the growth of your new Christian experience, be sure to break off any sinful relationship you may be in and get rid of anything that would keep you under sin's control. In addition, feed your spiritual life **daily** by practicing these spiritual disciplines:

- Communicate with your heavenly Father in prayer.
- Read and study the Bible—esteeming it as the infallible revelation of God to man (for Bible study aids visit www. thebiblechannel.com and www.thestreamtv.com).
- Get involved in a church that teaches and preaches the Bible.
- Tell others about Jesus and what He's done for you.
- Have regular fellowship with other Christians.
- Most of all, love God with your whole being by pleasing Him in all that you do, and love your neighbor as yourself.[28]

Welcome to God's family! Now tell someone else about the wonderful treasures you have discovered!

ENDNOTES

1. John 4:31-34 (NIV)
2. Hebrews 7:27; 9:24-28; 10:12-14
3. Leviticus 17:11; Hebrews 9:22
4. Acts 4:12
5. Genesis 4:2-7
6. Matthew 26:28 (KJV); Hebrews 9:15
7. Luke 13:1-5; Acts 2:37-39; 26:20; Matthew 3:8
8. John 6:28-29
9. John 8:24 (NIV)
10. John 3:16, 36; Mark 1:15; Hebrews 3:12-19; 11:6; Jude 1:5; Acts 16:31; Luke 18:17
11. 1 Corinthians 6:19

12. John 3:3-8

13. John 1:12; 3:3; Revelation 3:20; Matthew 10:37-40; James 2:5; John 15:1-10, 16

14. Romans 10:9-10; 6:3-6; Mark 16:16; Acts 2:38; 1 John 4:15; and Matthew 10:32-33

15. Colossians 1:10 (KJV)

16. Luke 9:23-25

17. Martin R. DeHaan II, *Our Daily Bread* (Radio Bible Class, 4/9/1990). Used by permission.

18. Philippians 1:6

19. Matthew 7:21-23; Luke 9:23-25; Romans 8:1, 4, 13-14; 2 Corinthians 6:15-18; Galatians 5:19-25; Colossians 3:3-15; 1 Timothy 4:1; Hebrews 6:4-6; 10:26-31; 12:14-15; 2 Peter 2:20-22; Revelation 2:7, 11, 17, 26; 3:5, 12, 15-16, 21

20. Matthew 13:44

21. Colossians 2:2-3

22. Romans 6:23; Ephesians 2:8-9

23. Revelation 3:20 (NIV)

24. Matthew 11:28 (NIV)

25. 2 Peter 3:9

26. Revelation 20:12-15; 21:27

27. 2 Corinthians 5:17

28. Matthew 22:36-40; Acts 2:41-42

·

ILLUSTRATION CREDITS

CHAPTER 2

Page 13, photo of man laying hand on animal, courtesy of Zola Levitt Ministries. Used by permission.

Page 18, map of Jerusalem, by permission of Mayo Foundation for Medical Education and Research. All rights reserved. William D. Edwards, J. Gabel Wesley, Floyd E. Hosmer, "On the Physical Death of Jesus Christ," *Journal of the American Medical Association*, (March 21, 1986), 255: 1456. Map sites renumbered with permission.

CHAPTER 3

Page 25, "Jesus Prays in the Garden." Public Domain. Retrieved on 4/22/2009 from www.karenswhimsy.com/public-domain-images/jesus-of-nazareth/jesus-of-nazareth-2.shtm

CHAPTER 5

Page 38, "Jesus Before Pilate." Public Domain. Retrieved on 4/22/2009 from www.karenswhimsy.com/public-domain-images/jesus-of-nazareth/jesus-of-nazareth-3.shtm

CHAPTER 6

Page 52, photo of three crosses, © istockphoto.com/Liliboas

Page 55, illustration of lunar eclipse, by Mary Anne Skeba.

CHAPTER 8

Pages 73-74, illustration of nailed hand and nailed foot, by permission of Mayo Foundation for Medical Education and Research. All rights reserved. William D. Edwards, J. Gabel Wesley, Floyd E. Hosmer, "On the Physical Death of Jesus

Christ," *Journal of the American Medical Association*, (March 21, 1986), 255: 1459-1460. Used by permission.

CHAPTER 9

Page 82, line drawing of Christ on the cross: Dynamic Graphics, Inc. © 1979.

CHAPTER 11

Page 92, photo depicting Jesus on the cross, © istockphoto.com/Liliboas

Page 97, illustration of a firebreak, by Mary Anne Skeba.

CHAPTER 13

Page 108, photo of Jewish temple, by James W. Watts, © 1998. Used by permission.

Page 108, diagram of Old Testament temple, by Mary Anne Skeba.

Page 112, photo of Gentile warning inscription, courtesy of Tchinly-Kosk Museum, Constantinople.

CHAPTER 14

Page 122, photo of bird, © istockphoto.com/lisafx

Page 126, illustration of spear in side, by permission of Mayo Foundation for Medical Education and Research. All rights reserved. William D. Edwards, J. Gabel Wesley, Floyd E. Hosmer, "On the Physical Death of Jesus Christ," *Journal of the American Medical Association*, (March 21, 1986), 255: 1462. Used by permission.

CHAPTER 15

Page 131, line drawing of Christ's feet crushing Satan's head, entitled "Genesis 3:15: The Promise Fulfilled," courtesy of Jim Kessler (www.InChristVictorious. com), accessed July 2007. Used by permission.

Page 133, photo of empty tomb, © istockphoto.com/McIninch

CHAPTER 17

Page 160, illustration of key in lock, by Mary Anne Skeba.

OTHER RESOURCES BY DAVID SKEBA

THE ARMOR OF GOD:
WINNING THE INVISIBLE WAR

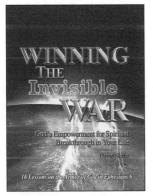

Lessons: 16 (24 sessions)
Dimensions:
Album: 11.5" x 13.5" x 2"
ISBN-13: 978-1-5589-7626-9
Workbook: 8.5" x 11" x 1.5"
Pages: 360 (Workbook)
ISBN-13: 978-0-7684-3112-4

Consists of a workbook and 4 DVDs—
a 7-hour video course.
Workbooks can be sold separately.
Each of the 16 DVD lessons is approx.
25 min.

The Former TV Series Is Now on DVD

There is a **mighty spiritual war** raging all around us. You have sensed it, felt it, and hoped it wasn't quite so real. It's all happening; right here, right now, in YOUR life.

We are being attacked from all fronts, and many of us don't know who our enemies really are or how to fight them. We have become the targets. We are the prize. **The battle is for our very souls—and for the glory of God!** What you don't know can hurt you.

Open your eyes and discover an invisible world you never knew existed. Learn how to fight and conquer enemies you cannot see—**your sinful nature, the world, and the devil**—so that you can victoriously finish your journey on earth and then live with God forever.

Using more than one thousand scripture references, this in-depth study explains all the pieces of **armor in Ephesians 6 and gives practical application on how to use them.** It's a survival guide to living victoriously on planet earth in these perilous end times. **God will empower you** to overcome all of your enemies and will **produce spiritual breakthrough** in your life and church.

Ways to Use It:

- Your own personal enrichment
- For home study groups
- For Sunday school or midweek services

Lesson Handouts and Quarterly Exams are also available

Available at www.DiscoverMinistries.com

Or Call (866) 55-DISCOVER

DISCOVER THE BIBLE ONLINE COURSES

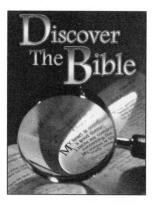

Have you ever wanted to learn more about the Bible but felt that taking an accredited college course was just not possible—perhaps due to lack of time to devote to it, its high cost, or because it is too scholarly, intimidating, and labor intensive?

Did you ever wish that simplified Bible courses were available to fit your busy schedule? Do you have an interest in taking courses that are brief in duration (from 4 to 8 lessons) and that average 30 minutes per lesson, as well as minimal in cost? Then *Discover the Bible* online courses are for you.

In an effort to make it easier for you to learn more about God and the Bible, and to meet the critical need of addressing biblical illiteracy in our day, we are offering **non-accredited** Bible courses on DiscoverMinistries.com within the *Discover the Bible* section. These online courses will be targeted for Christians at the Beginner, Intermediate, and Advanced levels.

Some of the courses will require a textbook to be purchased, but many courses will simply use the Bible. Check it out at **www.DiscoverTheBible.net**, and try our **free sample**.

About the Author

David and his wife, Mary Anne, have been married for over twenty-five years. An avid student of the Bible, David continues to search for effective ways to communicate God's Word in simple, practical ways. For more about David Skeba, visit his website at www.DiscoverMinistries.com and click on "About Us."

To order more copies of
Treasures from the Cross, go to
www.DiscoverMinistries.com

Or call toll-free (866) 55-DISCOVER.